SHERLOCK HOLMES:
FACT or FICTION?

SHERLOCK HOLMES: FACT or FICTION?

T. S. BLAKENEY

OTTO PENZLER BOOKS

New York

First published in 1932 by John Murray, London

Otto Penzler Books, 129 W. 56th Street,
New York, NY 10019 (Editorial Offices Only)

Macmillan Publishing Company, 866 Third Avenue,
New York, NY 10022

Maxwell Macmillan Canada, Inc., 1200 Eglinton Avenue East,
Suite 200, Don Mills, Ontario M3C 3N1

Macmillan Publishing Company is part of the Maxwell Communication Group of Companies.

Library of Congress Cataloging-in-Publication Data
Blakeney, T. S. (Thomas S.)
    Sherlock, Holmes : fact or fiction? / T.S. Blakeney.
      p.   cm.
    "First published in 1932 by John Murray, London"—T.p. verso.
    Includes bibliographical references.
    ISBN 1-883402-10-7
    1. Doyle, Arthur Conan, Sir, 1859–1930—Characters—Sherlock Holmes. 2. Detective and mystery stories, English—History and criticism. 3. Holmes, Sherlock (Fictitious character) 4. Private investigators in literature. I. Title.
PR4624.B6   1993   93-1799   CIP
823'.8—dc20

10 9 8 7 6 5 4 3 2 1

Printed in the United States of America

PREFACE

THIS essay is not intended for those who have never read or heard of Sherlock Holmes. Still less is it designed to supply in tabloid form a description of Holmes's cases for that section of the public that will not read the original texts. But for those who have at least a nodding acquaintance with Dr. Watson's writings, it is hoped that the following pages may prove acceptable, not only as revealing hidden depths in Holmes's life and character, but as correcting inaccuracies and throwing light on some obscurities. And, since we are nothing if not bibliographical nowadays,[1] I have thought it well to ' document ' the work somewhat thoroughly, the more so as past essays on the subject have suffered from insufficient annotation.

To the inevitable criticism that this study is not exhaustive, I would reply that it is not intended to be such. The time is not yet ripe. This work is an Introduction to studies, not a Critical Commentary on Holmes. It aims only at breaking the ground, at preparing the way and making a few paths straight. Research into the problems pre-

[1] M. R. James, *Collected Ghost Stories*, preface, p. ix.

sented by the life of Holmes has not yet reached the condition when a ' Handbook to Sherlock Holmes Studies ' can be usefully produced. The genealogist has yet to divulge his pedigree and to locate his place of birth ; the psycho-analyst has yet to plumb the depths of his subconscious mind. Little has been written, either here or elsewhere, about the Holmes-Watson friendship ; here is a fruitful field for the psychologist. His friends and associates have to be identified ; his daily itineraries described. Not until the Government archives are thrown open to the student to a much later date than at present obtains, can we hope to discern the part played by Mycroft Holmes in British politics of the later nineteenth century. It is indeed to be regretted that Messrs. Gooch and Temperley, in editing the British Documents on the origins of the Great War, did not commence, as is the case with the German and French publications, with the year 1871, for evidences of Mycroft would surely then have been found, thus rendering the volumes doubly valuable.

What is now required is, on the one hand, a series of detailed monographs on Holmes's cases, and on the other, deep investigation of the man's personality, his beliefs, his fads, his inconsistencies. At the same time, the literary critic must turn his mind to the perplexities involved in Watson's writings. We should welcome a critic who would grapple with this task as Mr. J. M. Robertson tackles Shakespearean problems, sifting the wheat from the chaff, the accretions of the pseudo-Watson (to say nothing of deutero- or trito-Watsons) from the core of matter deriving solely from the hand of the veritable John Henry. Fr. Ronald Knox has, in this connection, made important suggestions,[1] and my own views are given in the body of this work (pp. 37–43). It seems clear that the stories have been 'touched up', but the identification of the editors (for it would be inconsistent with the known characteristics of literary forgery that there should be only one) has yet to be made. Composite authorship may generally be attributed to historical writings, irrespective of whether the original record was the work of the putative author or of another person of the same name ; and the suggestion arises that the ' James ' Watson spoken of in *The Man with the Twisted Lip* may be one of these editors. Furthermore, since we thus have a ' James-John ' association, it seems inferentially probable (and surely not exegetically extravagant) that a ' Peter ' may also be looked for. The student who can discover amongst the friends, relatives or executors of Dr. Watson a James or a Peter may be on the way to a solution of the difficulties presented by Watson's work.

These suggestions are thrown out merely to in-

[1] *Essays in Satire*, p. 155.

dicate that there is still ample room for further investigations on Holmes ; when the researches have been accomplished it may then be time for one comprehensive mind to gather the results together into a ' Prolegomenon to any future Study of Sherlock Holmes '. In the meantime, I trust the present work will supply some wants and prove useful in initiating further efforts which should put in an assured setting the life and work of our distinguished countryman.

CONTENTS

MR. SHERLOCK HOLMES

IT has been claimed that great friendships between man and man present themselves to us with an inevitability comparable only to the time-honoured association of ham and eggs.[1] The breaking of such partnerships (whether of foodstuffs or of human material) is synonymous with the reign of chaos.[2] It will surely be allowed that the relationship of Sherlock Holmes and Dr. Watson belongs to this order ; we cannot think of one without envisaging the other ; we can hardly think of the time when either was not ; their names are interlocked with the history of crime with a certainty that surpasses the fleeting notoriety of a Wensley and beats Edgar Wallace all to nothing.

' I am lost without my Boswell ', says Holmes,[3] and whilst he undoubtedly had it in him to make his name famous in any event,[4] it is equally certain that he would not have become a household word the world over but for the stimulating influence and literary craftsmanship of his faithful satellite.   There

---

[1] P. G. Wodehouse, *The Clicking of Cuthbert*, p. 33.
[2] W. S. Gilbert, ' Princess Ida ', Act. II.
[3] *A Scandal in Bohemia*.   [4] *A Study in Scarlet*.

I

have been other friendships of a like nature in the detective world, but Holmes and Watson are the prototype of all such enduring partnerships. Eclipse is the first and the rest nowhere—it is to no purpose to try and compare the pale reflections presented to us in other memoirs with the one association present to every mind in such connections.

And just as surely as Holmes and Watson are linked together in inseparable conjunction, so also have they—and the first-named particularly— stamped their personalities with ineradicable persistence upon the drab surroundings of Baker Street.[1] Only in Fleet Street can we claim to find a thoroughfare permeated in an equal degree with the aura of a great individual ; and it is a measure of the position won by Holmes among Englishmen that he can be spoken of in the same breath as the great Doctor.

The date of Holmes's entry into the world is nowhere definitely given, but by the aid of his own process of ' reasoning analytically ', we can fix the occasion with fair precision. Altamont, alias Holmes, was, we are told, a man of sixty years of age in 1914,[2] but in this case we depend on the hand of an editor, and should be cautious of accepting the statement as more than a round figure,

[1] Cp. *Times Literary Supplement*, 16th April, 1931, p. 301, quoting A. St. John Adcock, ' London Memories ', p. 270 *seq.*
[2] *His Last Bow.*

which gives us merely an approximate guide. At the time of *The 'Gloria Scott'*, Holmes was at college ; let us say he was aged about twenty-one. He remained only two years at the University, when he came up to London, and *The Musgrave Ritual* (one of his earliest cases after the adoption of his career) was roughly four years later.[1] Now we are told that his career before the public lasted twenty-three years [2] : 1894–1903, both years inclusive, gives ten of these ; 1891–94 were years in which he was believed dead ; the remaining thirteen cover 1878–90. If, therefore, we place *The Musgrave Ritual* in 1878, Holmes would have come up to London in '74, and *The 'Gloria Scott'* would fall, say, in '73.[3] Deducting twenty-one years, and we reach 1852 as the year of his birth. We are probably safe in thinking that an earlier date is inadmissible ; but, on the other hand, 1853 is possible, as he might not be more than twenty at the time of *The 'Gloria Scott'*. Either of these years agrees sufficiently well with the declared age of Altamont, and an additional check is provided. Vernet, the French artist, was a granduncle of Holmes, and was born in 1789.[4] On the basis of this date, we

---

[1] He had known Reginald Musgrave at college, but had not seen him for four years.

[2] *The Veiled Lodger*.

[3] See below, p. 47, for further consideration of *The 'Gloria Scott'* chronology.

[4] *Nouvelle Biographie Generale*, xlvi, art. ' Vernet '.

should expect to find Holmes's mother marrying about 1840–45—say 1843. Mycroft Holmes was seven years the senior of Sherlock,[1] and should therefore have been born about 1845, which accords well with the estimated date of their mother's marriage. The only other relative we know of is Dr. Verner (whose name, as Mr. Roberts suggests, is possibly a corruption of Vernet), a distant relation who bought Watson's practice in Kensington about June 1894.

Of Holmes's school life we know nothing, but he duly entered one of the universities. As his bent was for chemistry, Cambridge would seem the most likely, especially seeing that his friend Trevor, being a Norfolk man, would more probably choose Cambridge, being geographically so near his home. Fr. Knox's dutiful claims in favour of Christ Church, Oxford, will not bear examination. The objection he raises, also, that Trevor's bulldog, whose biting of Holmes led to their acquaintance, would not have been allowed within the gates at the university, is invalid, as we are not told that Holmes was within college gates at the time. He was on his way to chapel, and was perhaps bitten in the town. He was only two years at college, and it is likely that at the time of the incident lived out.

It is fair, however, to say that London has claims to Holmes's student days. At the time of the ' Gloria Scott ' case he had rooms in town, possibly

[1] *The Greek Interpreter.*

4

the same as he was occupying in Montague Street some years later.[1] During the long vacation, he did chemical research in London [2] ; as late as 1881 he was utilizing the laboratories at Bart's.[3] We incline to the belief that Holmes was a Cambridge man who did not stay his full time,[4] but preferred to gravitate to London where he could pursue more easily his desultory studies. He speaks of ' coming up ' to London,[1] seemingly after leaving the 'Varsity, and settling down to a career—this surely indicates that hitherto he had dwelt mainly elsewhere.

On the paternal side Holmes was descended from English country squires.[5] Apparently it was from the alliance with the Vernet family that we trace the strong artistic element in Sherlock, exhibiting itself in him, apart from his flair for detection, as an interest in painting (however limited his knowledge),[6] a real talent for music, and a genius for

---

[1] *The Musgrave Ritual.*   [2] *The ' Gloria Scott '.*

[3] *A Study in Scarlet.*

[4] If we may take ' Camford ', the scene of the strange affair of the Creeping Man, as being a somewhat transparent *alias* for ' Cambridge ', we have additional reason for thinking Holmes hailed from the latter university, for he preserved happy recollections of ' an inn called the " Chequers " where the port used to be above mediocrity, and the linen was above reproach '. In *The Missing Three-Quarter*, also, he shows a knowledge of the countryside suggestive of former acquaintance.

[5] The name ' Sherlock ', however, suggests Irish associations.

[6] *The Hound of the Baskervilles*, and cp. *The Valley of Fear.*

histrionics.[1]   The latter qualities at first sight seem
a little at variance with the cold, calculating,
machine-like propensities which struck Watson so
forcibly, but the truth would seem to be that
here, as in other respects, Watson (a confirmed
sentimentalist) formed his opinion too lightly.
' Humanity and science in Holmes are strangely
blended ', remarks Fr. Ronald Knox.[2]   Young
Stamford thought him a little too scientific in his
tastes, but he hardly seems to have known Holmes
intimately.   The latter had a great capacity for
immersing his whole being in any particular study
in which he was concerned,[3] and at these times, no
doubt, he appeared wanting in other directions.
Scientific research was a passion with him,[4] and if
during experiments he was capable of testing the
effects of poison on a friend, or of flogging dead
bodies to see if bruises were produced (which con-
jures up an inimitable picture), such practices
testify to his absorption in his pursuit, but hardly
to a native inhumanity.   There are elements in
Holmes's character which suggest comparison with
the Duke of Wellington.[5]   In both, despite an out-

[1] See *The Sign of Four* (Athelney Jones's remarks) and *A Scandal
in Bohemia* (Watson's remarks).   [2] *Essays in Satire*, p. 174.

[3] See *The Sign of Four* (chemistry) and *The Bruce-Partington Plans*
(the Polyphonic Motets of Lassus).

[4] He speaks in *The Final Problem* of being prepared to retire and
devote his whole time to chemistry.

[5] Cp. J. W. Fortescue, *British Statesmen of the Great War*, pp. 241
seqq.

wardly cold aspect, we are vouchsafed glimpses of an emotional (not sentimental) nature kept in strong control, repressed, perhaps, from a sense that any display was a sign of weakness. Both were keen musicians, and music is the most emotional of all the arts; both could be delightful with children, who instinctively know real from feigned affability.[1] The Iron Duke broke down seldom, but those breaks were very complete; the other side of Holmes's nature peeps through even less thoroughly, but not less certainly. Three times [2] was Watson to witness these displays, as touching himself, and once Lestrade.[3]

Holmes possessed a genuine, if occasionally mordant sense of humour, and Fr. Knox [4] has drawn attention to his taste for epigram—neither trait belongs properly to a calculating-machine. There is more than a suggestion of the artificial in Holmes's assumed indifference to Miss Morstan's personality; we surmise that he had even then discerned Watson's interest (he certainly had a day or so later), and was not above trailing his coat, knowing full well that his friend would rise to the bait. However he might claim never to be in-

---

[1] Witness Holmes with young Jack, son of Mordecai Smith, in *The Sign of Four*. The Baker Street Irregulars were, too, clearly devoted to their master.

[2] In *The Bruce-Partington Plans*, *The Devil's Foot* and *The Three Garridebs*.

[3] *The Six Napoleons.*   [4] Op. cit., p. 174 *seq.*

fluenced by his client's appearance, we have many examples of his being acutely alive to their characteristics. He instantly perceives in Miss Violet Smith a ' spirituality ' that comes from a musical disposition [1] ; he quickly reacts to the tedious earnestness of Mr. Grant Munro [2] ; though he ' disliked and distrusted the sex ', and treated his female clients with the impersonality of a doctor towards his patients, he had a gift for answering sympathetically to the needs of the moment, and showed a ' remarkable gentleness and courtesy in his dealings with women '. [3]

Nor was he wanting in mercy to male delinquents, where justice inclined towards leniency. He would do nothing to hamper the escape of Dr. Sterndale —' if the woman I loved had met such an end, I might act even as our lawless lion-hunter has done ' [4] ; he treated the ex-bushranger and murderer John Turner with marked gentleness [5] ; he was moved by the tragic story of Browner [6] ; his sympathies were with the murderer of Charles Augustus Milverton, and he would not handle the case. More than once he refused to hand over a criminal to the police—' I suppose that I am commuting a felony, but it is just possible that I am saving a soul ' [7] ;

[1] *The Solitary Cyclist.*   [2] *The Yellow Face.*
[3] See *The Red Circle, Abbey Grange, Veiled Lodger, Speckled Band, Dying Detective,* etc.
[4] *The Devil's Foot.*   [5] *The Boscombe Valley Mystery.*
[6] *The Cardboard Box.*   [7] *The Blue Carbuncle.*

he would rather play tricks with the law of England than with his own conscience.[1] Watson never saw him more deeply moved than by the news of John Openshaw's death [2] ; he was stirred to a generous indignation by the callous conduct of Mr. Windibank [3] ; his behaviour to the Veiled Lodger is a good instance of the warmer nature that underlay a cold exterior.

In appearance hawklike and arresting, with aquiline nose and sharp, piercing eyes, Holmes must have presented a striking contrast to his bluff companion. Six feet in height or more, but ' so excessively lean that he seemed to be considerably taller ',[4] with a prominent, square-cut jaw, and a general atmosphere of keenness and alertness to all that was going on around him, he none the less at times exhibited an air of indolence and boredom that may well have been trying to an interviewer.[5] He accused himself of being ' the most incurably lazy devil that ever stood in shoe leather ',[4] and no doubt he was when he had no work on hand, for he seldom took exercise for exercise's sake, and regarded aimless bodily exertion as a waste of energy.[6] Yet he was essentially a man of action, not an arm-chair reasoner ; the latter was his

[1] *The Abbey Grange.*   [2] *The Five Orange Pips.*
[3] *A Case of Identity.*   [4] *A Study in Scarlet.*
[5] See *A Scandal in Bohemia* and *The Hound of the Baskervilles* (interviews with the King and Dr. Mortimer).
[6] *The Yellow Face.*

brother Mycroft's rôle, but not his. Few men were capable of greater muscular effort, and had Dr. Grimesby Roylott ever seen him in ' one of those outflames of nervous energy which could make him on occasion both the most active and the strongest man ' [1] Watson had ever known, he might have altered his method of introducing himself to a man whose grip was hardly inferior to his own. [2]

Holmes's strength was the strength of a steel spring, not of a sledge-hammer. When he boldly ventured forth in London with ' a huge barb-headed spear ' in his hand, and essayed to transfix a swung pig with a single blow of his weapon, he could not accomplish the task. [3] But in tireless pursuit of an objective he could have had few peers. Distance to be travelled, discomforts to be endured —these were things of no moment to him : food counted for little, and sleep less. Dawn was just breaking when Watson awoke after a short night's sleep before embarking on the investigation of the Priory School affair, but Holmes had already been out and about. He does not appear to have slept for some days while following up the Sholto murder. Sir Henry Baskerville and Watson were early afoot on the tremendous day that brought the former's dangers to a close, but Holmes had already been out on the moor, and effected the preliminary arrangements for the day's labours. Hard work

[1] *The Valley of Fear.*   [2] *The Speckled Band.*   [3] *Black Peter.*

never broke him down, but the aftermath was liable to leave him ' as limp as a rag for a week ' [1] ; ' and at a time when Europe was ringing with his name, and when his room was literally ankle-deep with congratulatory telegrams ', Watson could find him a prey to the deepest depression. [2] The immense strain to which his nervous energy was so frequently subjected made him, not altogether unnaturally, the ' self-poisoner by cocaine and tobacco ' [3] that so offended Watson's medical conscience, but he rose superior to the ' black reaction ' that his drug-taking involved, and never allowed his constitution to become undermined. When fleetness of foot alone could save Sir Henry Baskerville from the ' frightful thing ' which was hunting him down, Holmes could run as Watson (no mean judge) never saw a man run before or after ; and what better proof of the integrity of his nerve could be found than the momentous climb up the rock-wall above the Reichenbach Fall after the breathless struggle on the brink of the precipice had ended in the overthrow of Professor Moriarty ?

Of his other accomplishments we have varied evidence. He was an excellent boxer (he evidently gave McMurdo, the professional, a good fight,[1] and we all know what he did to Woodley),[4] a singlestick-player and swordsman,[5] and a sound wrestler with

---

[1] *The Sign of Four.*   [2] *The Reigate Squires.*   [3] *The Five Orange Pips.*
[4] *The Solitary Cyclist.*   [5] *A Study in Scarlet.*

some knowledge of baritsu or the Japanese method.[1]
He had a considerable knowledge of anatomy and
other scientific subjects, though it did not extend to
the mathematical and astronomical sciences so
popular to-day.[2] His knowledge of chemistry is
briefly summed up as ' profound '. It is interesting
to note, also, that although we cannot see Holmes
as much of a drawing-room man, he could if need
be take a hand at whist.[3] The contrast between
his neat, systematic methods of thought, as well
as his catlike love of cleanliness, and his exceedingly
untidy habits of life, is admirably portrayed for us
in *The Musgrave Ritual*, as also the occasional re-
volver practice indoors, which testified to his remarkable skill with fire-arms.[4] He early showed an
aptitude for detection, but it was chance that turned
his abilities into a profession.

As Fr. Knox has pointed out,[5] Watson was badly
at fault in his diagnosis of Holmes's limits of knowledge [6] ; Holmes was widely read, and had many
subjects at his fingers' ends, as evidenced by his
numerous quotations from various authors, English
and foreign, and by his conversational capacity on
several occasions.[7] Nor was he unwilling to learn,

[1] *The Empty House.* [2] *A Study in Scarlet.*
[3] *The Red-Headed League.* [4] See also *The Dying Detective.*
[5] *Essays in Satire*, p. 168 *seq.*
[6] *A Study in Scarlet* ; and cp. *The Five Orange Pips.*
[7] *The Sign of Four, The Greek Interpreter* ; also *The Hound of the Baskervilles* (painting) ; *The Cardboard Box* (music).

for whilst in *A Study in Scarlet* he did not know of Carlyle, by the time of *The Sign of Four* he evidently had more than a nodding acquaintance with his writings. Indeed, Holmes did not live up to his preaching about not storing the mind with unnecessary material ; he later extols ' the oblique uses of knowledge '[1] for their good results, and of such knowledge he had more than an average stock.[2] He must have known Latin, for no student of Early English charters can go far without that prerequisite of medieval research.[3] For the same investigations he must have known something of court-hand, and he had written a monograph on the dating of documents.[4] On another occasion we find him deep in a fifteenth-century palimpsest which had no bearing on nineteenth-century crime.[5] Indeed, the further our acquaintance with Holmes goes, the more we are struck by the manysidedness of his intellectual interests.

His philosophical outlook was rationalistic ; as a logician and precise thinker, he would naturally tend to place reason on the highest pinnacle, and we know that he regarded Winwood Reade's *Martyrdom of Man* as one of the most remarkable books ever written. Watson at first acquaintance declared that his knowledge of philosophy was nil,

[1] *The Valley of Fear.*　　　　　　　　[2] *The Lion's Mane.*
[3] C. G. Crump, *History and Historical Research*, p. 44.
[4] *The Hound of the Baskervilles.*　　　　[5] *The Golden Pince-nez.*

but in the preface to *His Last Bow* he speaks of Holmes, when in retirement, as dividing his time between philosophy and agriculture. He had read Darwin, for he quotes him on the subject of the influence of music in the animal world [1]; the significance of man in his relation to nature [2] and the purpose of his daily acts [3] were matters not lost upon 'the quiet thinker and logician of Baker Street.'[4] On more than one occasion we find him discussing Heredity with Watson, a subject in which he was evidently much interested.[5]

In other respects we find proofs of wide reading. The reference to the battles of Waterloo and Marengo in *The Abbey Grange* is very apt, and Holmes must surely have devoted some attention to Napoleonic history, for the remark was not one to occur to anybody. He carries a pocket Petrarch for reading on the railway,[4] and the range of his quotations is considerable. Goethe and Jean Paul are laid under contribution, and Richter referred to [2]; he compares Hafiz with Horace [6]; quotes Gustave Flaubert [7] and Thoreau.[8] He and Watson

---

[1] *A Study in Scarlet* : Darwin's remarks referred to are, apparently, those in *The Descent of Man*, pp. 86 *seq.*, 566 *seqq.* (pagination of the second edition).

[2] *The Sign of Four*.　　　　　[3] *The Cardboard Box.*

[4] *The Boscombe Valley Mystery.*

[5] See *The Greek Interpreter* and *The Empty House.*

[6] *A Case of Identity.*　　　　[7] *The Red-Headed League.*

[8] *The Noble Bachelor.*

discuss George Meredith rather than the perplexities of the Boscombe Valley case ; Tacitus and Shakespeare are quoted without acknowledgment.[1] His Biblical knowledge he admitted to be rather rusty,[2] but he quotes Ecclesiastes (i. 9) and probably had as good an acquaintance with the Bible as most men to-day.

He was not above the material comforts of this world, though he could dispense with them to an exceptional degree if need be.[3] He found a whisky-and-soda and a cigar a comfort after Lord St. Simon's visit, and furnished an excellent supper, cold but capital, for the Moultons. The dinner prior to the chasing of Jonathan Small was clearly a very happy affair, embellished by ' something a little choice in white wines '. He could appreciate Italian cooking,[4] and wisely chose Simpson's for the solid fare needed after prolonged abstinence.[5] His capacity to go without food was remarkable—Watson had known him, when occupied on a difficult case, to faint from exhaustion due to lack of nourishment.[6]

[1] Fr. Knox regards these quotations as evidence of the spurious character of ' The Return ' series, since ' he quotes Shakespeare in these stories alone '. As well regard *The Red-Headed League* as fictitious, since only there is Tacitus quoted. In point of fact, Holmes quotes Shakespeare also in *The Red Circle*.

[2] *The Crooked Man*, and cp. *The Valley of Fear.*

[3] Witness his spell on Dartmoor in *The Hound of the Baskervilles.*

[4] *The Bruce-Partington Plans.*   [5] *The Dying Detective.*

[6] *The Norwood Builder.*

But it is his musical talent that is his outstanding quality. He seems to have appreciated all forms of music, though the violin was his principal *forte*. He could play pieces, and difficult pieces, says Watson, but generally he sought solace in improvised airs, for which, indeed, he had a remarkable gift.[1] About the year 1888 he became the possessor of a Stradivarius, for the sum of only fifty-five shillings.[2] He was always willing to find the time to visit a concert, even during the midst of an investigation. More than once does Watson dwell upon Holmes's ability to switch his mind off his work, and find refuge in his favourite hobby : he turns quickly from the body of Gorgiano of the Red Circle to attend a Wagner night at Covent Garden ; Norman Neruda's concert is an antidote to the grim details of Drebber's murder ; he spends the whole afternoon before the finale of *The Red-Headed League* in St. James's Hall ; the problem of the *Cardboard Box* is forgotten in a feast of anecdotes of Paganini, and he and Watson celebrate the conclusion of the Baskerville mystery with a box for ' Les Huguenots ', with the De Reszkes performing. In *A Study in Scarlet* Watson complains of the aimless violin-playing, but these early pages from his journal seem to have been as hastily written as their opinions were hastily conceived. Thus, Holmes

[1] See *A Study in Scarlet* and *The Sign of Four.*
[2] *The Cardboard Box.*

is described as leaning back in his arm-chair, scraping at the fiddle thrown across his knee. The pose suggests difficulties in the matter of the fingering, and seems prohibitive for the double-stopping required for the production of chords. The whole description hardly agrees with the more mature opinion of him as ' a composer of no ordinary merit '.[1]

His philosophical outlook has already been referred to, and we do not know if he professed any religious views. It seems clear that he believed in a future existence,[2] and the idea that the universe might be ruled by chance was to him unthinkable.[3] But these beliefs do not belong only to religion, but are common to idealistic philosophers, spiritualists and others who support no church. They do not warrant our attributing any religious creed to Holmes ; his high opinion of Winwood Reade is evidence, if anything, to the contrary, as, also, is the place he assigns in a scale of values to the faculty of reason. The circumscribed outlook of a sectary seems quite inconsistent with his wide range of vision, and he was too strong a realist to be an adherent of any creed that bases its hold on an appeal to the senses.

[1] *The Red-Headed League.*
[2] See his remark to the Veiled Lodger—' the ways of Fate are indeed hard to understand. If there is not some compensation hereafter, then the world is a cruel jest '.
[3] *The Cardboard Box.*

We have no information, either, on Holmes's
political convictions. Watson said his knowledge
of politics was feeble,[1] and the news of a revolution,
of a possible war, and an impending change of
government did not arouse his interest.[2] He knew
enough of the trend of European affairs to recognize
from a vague description the author of the letter
that gave rise to the mystery of *The Second Stain*,
but it was not, perhaps, a difficult task. It is hard
to believe that Holmes, who had so close a grip on
realities, could ever have taken much interest in the
pettinesses of party politics, nor could so strong an
individualist have had anything but contempt for
the equalitarian ideals of much modern sociological
theory. He would spare no pains, and accept any
responsibilities when working on a matter of national
moment,[3] and his patriotism may be gauged by his
abandonment of a well-earned retirement in 1912
for two years of hectic excitement and, we may
believe, grave personal risk, for the outwitting of
Von Bork, the most astute Secret Service man in
Europe.

Of his personal habits, we have already dilated
on his musical talents, and his smoking will be
referred to in another place. His drug-taking is

[1] *A Study in Scarlet.*   [2] See *The Bruce-Partington Plans.*
[3] Witness his burglary of Oberstein's house, and his readiness to
buy back the missing document in *The Second Stain* even if it meant
an addition to the income-tax.

well known, and became a serious menace to his health.[1] Watson succeeded in weaning him away from it, but did not flatter himself that the cure was permanent. None the less, we do not hear of the practice in the later years of Holmes's career, and as it was only a stimulus in the absence of a problem to solve, doubtless he no longer felt the need of it once he had retired. Watson at first acquaintance considered that his habits of life forbade such a notion as drug-taking, so we may assume that in 1881 the practice had not begun. By 1888, however, it was strongly pronounced, and probably lasted intermittently till as late as 1897.[1] It was a pernicious habit, but fortunately was lived down, and did no permanent injury.

Mention has been made of his histrionic powers, which exhibit themselves in his capacity for disguise and his sense of theatrical arrangement. It was as a plumber that he courted Milverton's housemaid; the King of Bohemia's difficulties called for his appearance in such varied rôles as a drunken-looking groom and a Nonconformist clergyman. More than once Watson failed to penetrate his disguise : it was as a wizened bibliophile that he came to make the dramatic ' return ' that threw his friend into a faint ; the ancient mariner of *The Sign of Four* passed the scrutiny of Athelney Jones as well ; the victim of opium,[2] the venerable Italian

[1] *The Devil's Foot.*   [2] *The Man with the Twisted Lip.*

priest,[1] the unkempt French *ouvrier* [2]—all had to introduce themselves to Watson to ensure recognition. We are told that on one occasion he masqueraded as an old woman,[3] and the character of a loafer was familiar to him.[4] In the art of imitating illness he was so adept as to think of writing a monograph on malingering,[5] and we all know of the famous fit into which he fell at a critical moment in *The Reigate Squires*, and the sprained ankle during the investigation of the Duke of Holdernesse's affairs.

In addition, he had a finely developed taste for dramatic surprise. This was apt to be secured at the expense of his client, and might range from the moderate excitement of Mr. Holder [6] or Mr. Trelawney Hope [7] to the collapse of Percy Phelps at the dishing-up of the Naval Treaty, or the terrible ordeal imposed upon Sir Henry Baskerville. But even more characteristic of Holmes was his love for the staging of some well-wrought-out artistic finale. The most famous was surely the revealing of the black pearl of the Borgias in the bust of Napoleon, but it was the same instinct that ' put their own devilish trade-mark ' upon the murderers of John Openshaw,[8] evicted the Norwood

---

[1] *The Final Problem.* [2] *Lady Frances Carfax.*
[3] *The Mazarin Stone.* [4] *The Beryl Coronet* and *Mazarin Stone.*
[5] See *The Dying Detective* ; also *The Resident Patient.*
[6] *The Beryl Coronet.* [7] *The Second Stain.*
[8] *The Five Orange Pips.*

Builder from his cunningly concealed lair, or charged the Duke of Holdernesse to his face with the criminal concealment of his own son.[1]

It is to this disposition that we can trace another highly distinctive trait. He himself tells us [2] that he had found it useful to impress a client with his sense of power, and two methods contribute to this effect. By the one, he exhibits his capacity ' by what the South Americans now call " Sherlockholmitos " ', which are clever little deductions on matters not directly connected with the concern in hand [3]; and by the other, in the casual references he throws out from time to time to other cases which a particular event brings to his mind. In the former class are the rapid reading of a client's character and profession, as in *The Red-Headed League*, *The Norwood Builder*, *The Blanched Soldier* and *The Speckled Band*, to say nothing of the interjectory remarks during the course of conversation that so startled the King of Bohemia, Mr. Grant Munro,[4] and Miss Mary Sutherland.[5] Watson himself was sometimes the victim of these feats of deduction, somewhat painfully in the matter of

[1] Holmes could appreciate a dramatic situation without its being his own production : the announcement of the murder at Birlstone (*The Valley of Fear*) was, we are told, one of those moments for which he existed.

[2] *The Blanched Soldier.*

[3] A. C. Doyle, *Memories and Adventures*, p. 126.

[4] *The Yellow Face.*   [5] *A Case of Identity.*

his brother's character, as revealed in his watch.[1] To the reader of the cases, however, the elucidation, for Watson's benefit, of the characteristics of Dr. Mortimer from his walking-stick,[2] Grant Munro from his pipe,[3] and the murderess at Yoxley Old Place from her spectacles,[4] will instantly occur, reaching a climax in the unforgettable duel between Mycroft and Sherlock Holmes in *The Greek Interpreter*, and (most masterly of all) the description of Mr. Henry Baker as proclaimed in the battered billycock hat.[5]

The second characteristic, that of casual mention of other cases, is less striking, but not less real. We see it noticeably in *A Study in Scarlet*, both in the string of cases he refers to which would have been effected by his newly-discovered blood test, and in the remark instantly made at the sight of Drebber's body to the affair in Utrecht in '34. Lestrade's story of the breaker of Napoleonic busts recalls to his mind ' the dreadful business of the Abernetty family ' which was first brought to his notice by the depth the parsley had sunk into the butter on a hot day [6] ; we should like very much to know more of ' the singular affair of the aluminium

[1] See also *Lady Frances Carfax, The Dancing Men, The Boscombe Valley Mystery,* and *A Scandal in Bohemia.*

[2] *The Hound of the Baskervilles.*   [3] *The Yellow Face.*

[4] *The Golden Pince-nez.*   [5] *The Blue Carbuncle.*

[6] We may compare a somewhat similar example in the career of Sergt. Cuff—see Wilkie Collins, *The Moonstone*, chap. xii.

crutch ', to say nothing of Ricoletti of the club-
foot and his abominable wife.[1] The collection of
M's in his great index of biographies was, we
know, a fine one,[2] and we hear also of some S's,
such as the Stauntons [3] and Bert Stevens.[4] Watson
even more than Holmes has this habit, and whets
our appetites by such titles as ' the repulsive story
of the red leech and the terrible death of Crosby
the banker ' [5]; ' the shocking affair of the Dutch
steamship, *Friesland* ' [4]; and the adventure of ' the
Amateur Mendicant Society, who held a luxurious
club in the lower vault of a furniture warehouse '.[6]
In the absence of fuller details, however, we must
rest content with the not inconsiderable feast
Watson has provided for us,[7] and to a detailed
study of Holmes's career we will shortly proceed.
Before doing so, however, we must make brief
reference to his relations with the official police
force, and enter into the question of the literature
dealing with the great detective.

[1] *The Musgrave Ritual.*   [2] *The Empty House.*
[3] *The Missing Three-Quarter.*   [4] *The Norwood Builder.*
[5] *The Golden Pince-nez.*   [6] *The Five Orange Pips.*
[7] We get a taste of what tales remain untold in Holmes's reminis-
cent reference (at the outset of *The Sussex Vampire*) to the case of
Matilda Briggs—' not the name of a young woman, Watson : it
was a ship which is associated with the giant rat of Sumatra, a story
for which the world is not yet prepared '. Cp. also Watson's opening remarks in *Thor Bridge* ; perhaps Holmes's failure over the
cutter *Alicia* decided him not to add to the number of would-be
solvers of the mystery of the *Mary Celeste*.

HOLMES AND SCOTLAND YARD

SHERLOCK HOLMES is nothing if not a contrast to
Scotland Yard. His reputation, indeed, has largely
been built up by the regularity of his successes over
the official force, successes due to his entirely different attitude towards the cases he investigated,
and to the original methods adopted in their solution. The Yard attitude was that of the promoted
policemen they were, and they looked at the art
of detection as Mr. Gradgrind looked at the teach-
ing of history. 'Now what I want is Facts. . . .
Facts alone are wanted in life. Plant nothing else,
and root up everything else. You can only form
the minds of reasoning animals upon facts ; nothing
else will ever be of any service to them. . . . Stick
to Facts, Sir.' Compare Athelney Jones, on his
entrance into the Sholto murder case : 'What is
all this ? Bad business ! Bad business ! Stern
facts here—no room for theories. . . .' The point
of view is the same in both instances, and the
parallel only breaks down at the difficulty of
likening Jones even to a reasoning animal !

But the imagination necessary for the proper
handling of the facts they accumulated was lack-

24

ing in the Scotland Yarders, and the want of it frequently led to their overlooking the really important data for their case. Stanley Hopkins could get his facts pretty clear ; all he wanted was to know what they meant ! [1] Even Athelney Jones could discover something, and Inspector Gregory, evidently one of the brightest representatives of the Yard, might have solved the mystery of Silver Blaze's disappearance had he possessed the imagination that was his one deficiency. Each and any of the Inspectors could do the mere spade-work of detection, such as searching for a given man : we see Lestrade working his way patiently through all the hotels of a district, [2] or dragging the Serpentine for dead bodies [3] ; although the really practical search for the murderer in the Boscombe Valley case he seemed to consider too much trouble.

The professionals were energetic enough, but they wasted their energies on irrelevant details, and one and all seemed unable to hit upon the central clue in a case. Gregson took offence in *A Study in Scarlet* when Holmes suggested there was a single clue (which they had overlooked) on which all else hinged ; Hopkins, though presented with the idea that the tobacco-pouch in the case of Black Peter should be the starting-point of the investigation, could not see it. Contrast Holmes. He possessed

---

[1] *The Golden Pince-nez.*   [2] *A Study in Scarlet.*
[3] *The Noble Bachelor.*

25

in a high degree the capacity to discern which, of a mass of details, were those really important. Just as the student must be able whilst reading to skip what is unnecessary to his work,[1] or a great judge see through a tangle of evidence to the heart of the case before him [2] ; just as Dr. Johnson could tear the heart out of a book in half an hour, or Macaulay take in a page of information almost at a glance, so Holmes instinctively fixed upon the crucial points of a case as it was being outlined to him. Thus, in *The Valley of Fear*, the significance of the single dumb-bell was hidden from all minds but his ; ' the curious incident of the dog in the night-time ' [3] ; the bees'-wing in only one wine-glass at the Abbey Grange ; the need of visiting the Blackheath home of John Hector MacFarlane before going to the scene of the supposed murder ; the true import of the Napoleonic busts—innumerable instances could be given of his intuitive insight into the meaning of the data laid before him. Watson was at first incredulous of Holmes's claim to be able to solve a mystery from his arm-chair,[4] but we have examples of his doing so, as in *A Case of Identity*, *The Red-Headed League*, and *The Noble Bachelor*.

Fr. Knox [5] has drawn attention to the contrast

---

[1] Cp. C. G. Crump, *History and Historical Research*, p. 81.
[2] Macaulay, *History of England*, chap. iv (*re* Judge Jeffreys).
[3] *Silver Blaze*.   [4] *A Study in Scarlet*.
[5] *Essays in Satire*, p. 147.

between Holmes's methods in laying by the heels the bank-smashers in *The Red-Headed League*, and the behaviour of Scotland Yard in the famous Houndsditch affair, and it is a contrast that exhibits in practice the dissimilarity of their reasoning processes in all detective work. The accredited representatives of the law might have the power of observation, and occasionally that of deduction, but they never succeeded in putting themselves in the criminal's place, and, by arguing what he would be most likely to do, arrange their plans to forestall him. In this art Holmes was a past-master, and it was a practice that served him well. In *A Study in Scarlet*, *The Sign of Four*, *The Musgrave Ritual*, *Silver Blaze*, this capacity for inductive reasoning—'reasoning analytically' as he called it—led to the true solution of the problem. 'You know my methods in such cases, Watson : I put myself in the man's place, and having first gauged his intelligence, I try to imagine how I should myself have proceeded under the same circumstances.' It is the mark of a great general that he can predict what his opponent is doing 'on the other side of the hill', and Holmes had this quality in a high degree. Occasionally it might degenerate into little more than guessing at events, as in his first diagnosis of the mystery of the Yellow Face,[1] but he kept his mind always alive to the possibility that he might be mistaken. 'It

[1] Other examples are *The Sign of Four* and *The Speckled Band*.

is a capital mistake to theorize before you have all the evidence. It biases the judgment.'[1] The advantage of keeping an open mind is well illustrated in his narration of the reasoning out of the mystery of *The Cardboard Box*. It is consistent, too, with his coldly logical disposition that he would admit his blunders instead of glossing over them. He mystified Watson in *The Valley of Fear* with strange comparisons of himself to 'a lunatic, a man with softening of the brain, an idiot whose mind has lost its grip'; the cases of *Lady Frances Carfax* and *The Man with the Twisted Lip* called forth similar self-reproaching; and in *A Study in Scarlet* he was stung to the one instance on record of his swearing—'old woman be damned; we were the old women to be so taken in'.

If baffled, he could sit down, review his evidence and reshuffle his ideas, and his pipe or his violin was a valuable aid to reflection. 'Having gathered these facts, Watson, I smoked several pipes over them'[2]; 'it is quite a three-pipe problem'[3]; these are characteristic sayings. The identity of the Man with the Twisted Lip was revealed to him in the smoke of an ounce of tobacco, whilst under the influence of 'a pound of the strongest shag' his spirit was conveyed from London to Dartmoor for a

---

[1] *A Study in Scarlet*; cp. *A Scandal in Bohemia* and *The Cardboard Box*.
[2] *The Crooked Man*.   [3] *The Red-Headed League*.

day. Not even Mr. Baldwin can surpass Holmes in his love for his pipe, though we trust he has not an equally coarse palate. Holmes smoked cigars and cigarettes at times, but these, we feel, were but impatient gestures in the smoking line ; his old and oily clay was to him as a counsellor,[1] though liable to be supplanted by the long cherrywood when in disputatious rather than meditative mood [2] : his before-breakfast smoke was loathsomely composed of the dried dottles of all his pipefulls of the day before.[3]

But to delineate in detail the ever-recurring contrast between Holmes's methods and those of Scotland Yard would be to epitomize the great bulk of his cases, a task that may properly be left to each student for himself. We must, however, touch upon his relationships with a few of the principal Inspectors.

In the main, though we meet with several members of the official force during the years 1881–1903 which cover Holmes's career as a detective, very seldom do we find one who is not dull-witted to the verge of imbecility in comparison with the great amateur. Inspector Baynes, of the Surrey Constabulary,[4] alone comes out of the ordeal with credit, and it is characteristic of Holmes that he very fully and promptly recognized the fact. ' You

---

[1] *A Case of Identity.*   [2] *The Copper Beeches.*
[3] *The Engineer's Thumb.*   [4] *The Adventure of Wisteria Lodge.*

will rise high in your profession,' he remarked ; ' you have instinct and intuition.' It is true Watson tells us that Holmes listened without impatience to White Mason on the occasion of the Birlstone mystery,[1] but eventually neither Mason nor Inspector Macdonald of Scotland Yard—who was himself to attain a national reputation in later years—contributed to the unravelling of the affair ; on the contrary, they were chided by Holmes not a little, and lost their tempers during the process. A number of others appear once only, such as Inspector Martin,[2] Inspector Gregory,[3] Inspector Forbes,[4] and Inspector Lanner,[5] but they leave no mark.

We learn that Inspector Stanley Hopkins was a young man upon whom Holmes had at one time based high hopes,[6] but there are signs that by November 1894 the pupil was beginning to show his inherent weaknesses,[7] and by July of the following year [6] he had caused the master considerable disappointment. Not without reason, either. Holmes was, it is true, an irritating and somewhat exacting exemplar, who suffered fools most ungladly,[8] but

---

[1] *The Valley of Fear.*   [2] *The Dancing Men.*
[3] *Silver Blaze.*   [4] *The Naval Treaty.*
[5] *The Resident Patient.*   [6] *Black Peter.*
[7] *The Golden Pince-nez.*
[8] *The Bruce-Partington Plans* : ' It was one of my friend's most obvious weaknesses that he was impatient with less alert intelligences than his own.'

though we may forgive Hopkins for confusing the initials of Patrick Cairns with those of Peter Carey, what are we to make of the invincible dullness that failed to read ' Canadian Pacific Railway ' into the letters C.P.R. ?

Hopkins does not appear frequently, and only in the years following ' The Return ', nor does he ever do himself much credit. ' What did you do, Hopkins, after you had made certain that you had made certain of nothing ? ' was Holmes's acid comment on his investigations in the affair of the Golden Pince-nez. Hopkins eventually realized, and promptly apologized for his ineptitude over the murder of Black Peter, but when we next meet him, two years later, he still exhibits that hopeless inflexibility of mind which prevents him from considering the possibility that it is the story of Lady Brackenstall that is wrong, and not the ' facts ' as he chooses to see them. ' There are other gangs of three ' is all he has to say, when his theories have collapsed about his ears, his suspected burglars having been located in another continent, and the supposed reason for their housebreaking been shown to be null and void.[1]

That Holmes was untouched by any sense of jealousy of another's abilities is exhibited in his appreciatory remarks on M. le Villard, who in 1888 was coming rapidly to the fore in France.[2] On the

[1] *The Abbey Grange.* [2] *The Sign of Four.*

other hand, he would admit of no one being his superior—witness his attitude to Dr. Mortimer's tactless praise of M. Bertillon.[1] At a time when he knew Watson but slightly, he refers to Gregson as ' the smartest of the Scotland Yarders ; he and Lestrade are the pick of a bad lot ',[2] but a few years later he speaks more freely of ' being out of their depths ' as their normal condition.[3] And indeed, so far as his remarks apply to Athelney Jones, nothing that Holmes ever said was too severe. Of all the incompetents who ever bungled a case, none strikes us so unfavourably as this vast and vacuous man, unaccountably promoted from the policeman's beat for which his heavy tread and unimaginative mind befitted him ; wheezing his way fatly through life, fortified only by a dull and animal vigour, and an abysmal stupidity that rendered him oblivious to anything higher than his own deficiencies.

Inspector Gregson meets us in early days, but, we feel, hardly maintained his (undeserved) reputation. We come across him again in *The Red Circle*, belonging apparently to the early eighties,[4] *The Greek Interpreter*, and the adventure of *Wisteria Lodge*, when he did nothing of value, but he never bulks very large after *A Study in Scarlet*. True, the newspapers,

---

[1] *The Hound of the Baskervilles*. Not that he despised Bertillon—on the contrary, he had an enthusiastic admiration for him—see *The Naval Treaty*.

[2] *A Study in Scarlet*.   [3] *The Sign of Four*.   [4] See below, p. 50.

with customary inaccuracy, heralded the capture
of Jefferson Hope as due to the abilities of Gregson
and Lestrade, but as Watson published the true
version of the affair in the next few years,[1] the
public soon learned of the poor showing of the
Yard detectives. Lestrade weathered the exposure
all right, but Gregson, who appears but little in
the future, was perhaps a scapegoat for the two of
them—not undeservedly, for he had contributed in
no way to the solution, whilst Lestrade had at
least discovered the murdered Stangerson, to say
nothing of the word ' Rache '.

It is of Lestrade that we naturally think as the
official coadjutor of Holmes. From 1881 [2] to
1895 [3] he is constantly in action, and if, as seems
likely,[4] *The Six Napoleons* and *Charles Augustus
Milverton* fall within the period 1896–1900, he must
in all have had some forty years' experience.[5] For
about half of this long career he was associated with
Holmes. Envious at first of his younger and un-
official rival,[6] in one of the last cases in which we
know the two were together, Lestrade paid tribute

---

[1] It had been brought out prior to *The Sign of Four*.
[2] *A Study in Scarlet*.   [3] *The Bruce-Partington Plans*.
[4] See below, p. 104.
[5] In *A Study in Scarlet* he speaks of his twenty years' experience.
If *The Three Garridebs* can be trusted on a point of detail, Lestrade
was still going strong in 1902.
[6] ' The old hound is the best ', he exclaims irritably in *A Study
in Scarlet*.

to Holmes in a handsome manner which genuinely touched the latter. 'We're not jealous of you at Scotland Yard,' he remarked ; ' No, sir, we are very proud of you, and if you come down to-morrow there's not a man, from the oldest inspector to the youngest constable, who wouldn't be glad to shake you by the hand.'[1]

Poor Lestrade ; he learned little by experience, and certainly never to think twice before assuming that his views were more accurate than those of Holmes. Like the luckless Spanish army before Napoleon, he suffers some cataclysmic defeat only to come up again at a later date to meet with another inevitable drubbing. Whether it is ' tapping his forehead significantly ' to indicate his opinion of the other [2] ; or exclaiming that views opposed to his own were ' the merest moonshine '[3] ; or advising Holmes to abandon a case [4] ; or un- hesitatingly propounding those wild shots in the dark which in him passed for deductions ; no matter what it is, he is constantly wrong, and the best that can be said for him is that he handled some cases with less than his usual . . . that is to say, he handled them fairly well.[5] Yet for old association's sake, we entertain a warm feeling for Lestrade ; he compares well with his fellow-

---

[1] *The Six Napoleons.*   [2] *The Noble Bachelor.*
[3] *The Boscombe Valley Mystery.*   [4] *The Norwood Builder.*
[5] *The Empty House.*

inspectors, on the whole : he is ready to stand by his own work, such as it is, instead of shuffling the responsibilities for his failures on to his associates, or sneering at his collaborators, as Gregson sneers at him.[1] Like Athelney Jones, he on occasion becomes insufferable [2] ; unlike him, he admits to his blunders, and in any case his impudence is of a more delicate nature, the vice losing half its evil by losing all its grossness. It is for this wiry, little bulldog of a man that Holmes sends at the crucial moment of ' the biggest thing for years ',[3] which is to be remembered to Lestrade's credit as sufficient of itself to mark him out from the common herd of Scotland Yard officials.

[1] See *A Study in Scarlet.*   [2] For example, in *The Norwood Builder.*
[3] *The Hound of the Baskervilles.*

THE LITERATURE RELATING TO
SHERLOCK HOLMES

It has been truly said that any studies in Sherlock Holmes are, first and foremost, studies in Dr. Watson.[1] It is on the basis of the latter's writings that any competent critique must rest. These writings fall into two divisions, those before and those after ' The Return '.

In the first division we have :—

(a) *A Study in Scarlet.*
(b) *The Sign of Four.*
(c) *The Hound of the Baskervilles.*
(d) *The Valley of Fear,*

all long, complete stories, and

(e) *The Adventures of Sherlock Holmes.*
(f) *The Memoirs of Sherlock Holmes.*

That these volumes are authentic writings of Watson there can surely be little question. Fr. Knox has, it is true, suggested doubts, only to rebut them. As regards *A Study in Scarlet*, this was written before 1888, as Watson and Holmes speak of it in *The Sign of Four*, though the fact that Holmes should say he had glanced over it, and speak

[1] Fr. Ronald Knox, *Essays in Satire*, p. 147.

generally as if it was a new subject of discussion, suggests that it had not long been in print. It is likely that Watson had published some of the earlier adventures before this date, since Mycroft Holmes refers to Sherlock's growing fame, thanks to Watson, at the time of *The Greek Interpreter*, which is probably before 1887.[1] Stapleton, too, in '89 remarks that Holmes's fame and Watson's association with him had penetrated even to Dartmoor, an event scarcely feasible had only *A Study in Scarlet* been in print. In *A Scandal in Bohemia* (1889) [2] Holmes refers to Watson having chronicled one or two of his cases, and by the time of *The Copper Beeches* (after 1889) he had written several at least of his stories, and perhaps still more by 1897, the date of the *Abbey Grange* mystery.

Neither *The Sign of Four* nor *The Hound of the Baskervilles* can seriously be impugned, and Fr. Knox makes short work of the suggestion that the latter was after 1903. *The Adventures* and *The Memoirs* seem universally accepted, nor has any doubt been thrown on *The Valley of Fear*.

A large and difficult question is whether these last-named records have suffered in any way from editorial ' touching up '. There are certain curious discrepancies that are only with considerable difficulty explicable as Watson's own. Thus, in *The*

[1] See below, p. 52.
[2] For a discussion of this date, see below, p. 59.

Man with the Twisted Lip, Mrs. Watson is made to
speak of her husband by the name of 'James',
whereas, of course, it was really 'John'. Could
Watson himself have made such a mistake? Again,
the original text [1] of *The Resident Patient* contained
the thought-reading incident also to be found in
The Cardboard Box. At first sight we might regard
The Cardboard Box as spurious, belonging as it does
to a volume which certainly owes something to
an editorial hand. But it will be observed that in
the latter version, the month is August, but October
in *The Resident Patient*, and it seems more natural
that Watson should be yearning for the shingle of
Southsea in August than in the later month. This
being the case, how came the incident in question
into *The Resident Patient* at all?

Once more, the adventure known as *The Second
Stain* is twice referred to in terms that have no
bearing on the story actually recorded. On the
one occasion Watson couples it with *The Yellow
Face* as an example of where Holmes, though mistaken in his deductions, none the less discovered the
truth during his investigation; on the other,[2]
Watson's remarks have no resemblance to the facts
of the case. The problem was a political one, but
not of high social significance, as is inferred; Holmes

---

[1] We say 'original' text, as the passage is quietly suppressed in
the collected (or 'omnibus') edition of Watson's works.

[2] *The Naval Treaty.*

had little room for the play of his great powers; the police, and most of all the foreign police, were kept out of it entirely, save in so far as Eduardo Lucas's death was concerned. Clearly some other case is in mind, but the title has been confused. Could Watson really make so many blunders as these? Is it possible to discern a third hand in all this? Perhaps not; but even if Watson was writing from memory alone, and without recourse to his note-books, we find it hard to understand how even he [1] could be so lax. We do not consider that the author's lapses or editor's emendations, as the case may be, invalidate the records, but whatever explanation is given, they justify us in accepting cautiously Watson's statements on points of detail.

It is with the stories of the second division that the greater difficulties commence. These are :—

(a) *The Return of Sherlock Holmes.*

(b) *His Last Bow.*

(c) *The Case Book of Sherlock Holmes.*

There are some who deny that Watson ever wrote these at all; others who believe that *The Final Problem* was faked by him, and that ' The

---

[1] We say ' even he ' advisedly, for we shall see later, e.g. in connection with *The Final Problem* and *The Red-Headed League*, that Watson was at times distressingly inaccurate. A further instance is in connection with his wound; in *A Study in Scarlet* he says he was struck on the shoulder, but in *The Sign of Four* the Jezail bullet rendered him lame !

Return' series is genuine.[1] Fr. Knox himself considers that Watson wrote 'The Return' stories (and presumably the others of later date) himself, but that the events they chronicle are untrue.[2] Mr. Roberts appears at one time to have entertained some doubts about *His Last Bow* and *The Case Book*,[3] and in his later work, 'Dr. Watson' (p. 28 with note), with commendable prudence, refuses to dogmatize on the canonicity of at least one story in *The Case Book*. Mr. A. A. Milne doubts the authenticity of the whole collection in the latter volume.[4]

For ourselves, we believe that all the stories record true events in the life of Holmes, but that the collections in *His Last Bow* and *The Case Book* come to us through the hand of an editor. This is certainly the case as regards the individual stories known as '*His Last Bow*' and '*The Mazarin Stone*', and there is further evidence.

His Last Bow contains cases taken from no special period of Holmes's career, but ranging from the eighties to as late as 1914. Now, although Watson in *The Memoirs* and *The Adventures* allows himself a fair latitude of time within the limits of which his stories fall, in each instance they cover less than ten years, and frequently occur within one or two. Thus, in *The Adventures*, the first seven stories are

---

[1] *Essays in Satire*, pp. 148–9, 150 *seqq.*   [2] *Id.*, p. 153 *seq.*
[3] *A Note on the Watson Problem*, p. 7.   [4] See *By Way of Introduction*.

all within a comparatively short time of Watson's marriage. In *His Last Bow*, however, the cases do not appear ever to be closely related in time, but by their great diversity of years suggest that an editor put together the compilation, choosing such stories as struck him most forcibly, picking them out from a number of Watson's MSS., and forming consequently a strikingly interesting but heterogeneous collection. He may have confined himself or been limited to stories that were virtually ready for the press, adding only the late adventure, ' *His Last Bow* ', from notes made by Watson. The latter had, it would seem, been engaged upon the task of collecting together some other records of Holmes's life, for he had a preface ready written. The Watsonian style is apparent in every case, even the last, and it is probably the not-too-skilful hand of the editor that has caused such blemishes as the recorded date of *Wisteria Lodge* (1892, when Holmes was travelling in Tibet !).

The *Case Book* is somewhat different. To the most superficial reader, the literary skill is much inferior to any other of Watson's writings, and there are, at best, only occasional glimpses of the old Holmes.[1] Our own belief is that a third hand has

[1] E.g. the remark that Bob Ferguson must not regard Baker Street as a home for the weak-minded seems redolent of the true Holmes, and the telegram he sent, summoning Watson to the investigation of *The Creeping Man* case, has an authentic ring : ' Come at once if convenient—if inconvenient come all the same. S. H.'

written up these cases from Watson's rough notes—
in two instances from Holmes's writings—and has
clumsily endeavoured to imitate Watson's style.
Thus, in *The Illustrious Client*, Holmes's insistence
on knowing the name of Colonel Damery's principal (when, in point of fact, he eventually chose to
forgo such knowledge save by indirect means)
looks like a poor imitation of the well-known
passage of arms with Lord Bellinger in *The Second
Stain*. His cheap jeers at the negro in *The Three
Gables* are quite inconsistent with his formal and
reserved behaviour, as repeatedly exhibited to us,
while it is impossible to believe him guilty of the
vulgarism of referring, before a woman, to Watson's
smoking as his ' filthy habits '.[1]   Again, his tirade
against Neil Gibson's morals [2] is quite contrary to
the impersonal attitude he habitually adopted
towards his clients,[3] and throughout the book his
conversation is very unlike that known to us from
authentic documents.   There are elements in *The
Mazarin Stone* (admittedly written by a third hand)
which suggest cribbing from a famous incident in
The Empty House ; it is gross carelessness to describe
an event in the list of contents as ' *The Adventure of
Shoscombe Abbey* ', but in the text as ' *Shoscombe Old
Place* ' ;   and only the most culpable ignorance
would cause Holmes to speak of the ' Abbey School '

[1] *The Veiled Lodger.*   [2] *Thor Bridge.*
[3] See, for example, *The Sign of Four.*

42

instead of the ' Priory School ', and the Duke of Greyminster instead of the Duke of Holder-nesse.

We have already indicated that Watson himself was not always accurate in points of detail. That slips should occur occasionally is but natural ; the cases were written up by him at various times, under diverse conditions, and sometimes years after the events they record. Nevertheless, there are rather serious inaccuracies to be found, that in-dicate a carelessness not wholly excusable. These errors being pointed out as they occur in the course of the chronological survey of Holmes's career, it is unnecessary to go further into them now.

A certain body of critical writings has already grown up round Sherlock Holmes and Watson, and it will be evident throughout this work to what extent we are indebted to them.

The essay by Fr. Ronald Knox [1] dates back some twenty years, and is based on only a portion of the whole *corpus* of Holmes-literature. *The Return of Sherlock Holmes* is dismissed after certain criticisms as being a fabrication, and *The Valley of Fear*, *His Last Bow*, and *The Case Book* are not considered.[2]

---

[1] ' Studies in the Literature of Sherlock Holmes ', in *Essays in Satire*, pp. 145-75.

[2] Inconsistently, however, he quotes, as an example of a special type of epigram, nicknamed the Sherlockismus, a saying from *The Devil's Foot*, which, of course, is outside the limits of his canon. There are other similar lapses.

As a pamphlet by Mr. S. C. Roberts [1] has dealt in some detail (although not exhaustively) with the errors which, we are sorry to say, abound in Fr. Knox's work, it is needless to pursue the matter further, beyond recording our opinion that the inaccuracies are due to his neglect of just those methods of critical investigation which it is the purpose of his book to decry. Apart from this, however, we express our keen enjoyment of his writing, which as a piece of literature must always rank high, and which manifests sound insight into the psychology of Holmes and Watson. We owe it to Fr. Knox that the latter's literary affinities with Plato and Æschylus have been made clear, and no one need hope to rival the art with which he has portrayed Watson for all time as the embodiment of bowler-hattedness. Indeed, there is less of Holmes than of his companion in this work : what we have of the former is both attractive and instructive, and we could wish the essay had been greatly prolonged.

There is an American pamphlet by F. D. Steele, [2] produced in honour of William Gillett, but it is not available as a rule to students in England, and is therefore passed over. Mr. A. A. Milne, in his

---

[1] 'A Note on the Watson Problem.' (We are greatly indebted to Mr. Roberts for a copy of this essay, which is not generally obtainable.)

[2] *Sherlock Holmes.*

volume *By Way of Introduction*, has an essay on Holmes, provoked by the appearance of *The Case Book*, which, he pleads, is spurious. He is misled, however, by his failure to realize that it was of Watson's second marriage that Holmes was writing in *The Blanched Soldier*, and his criticisms therefore do not apply.

An exceedingly interesting study of ' The Adventure of the Three Students ' has been written by Mr. Vernon Rendall in his work, *The London Nights of Belsize* : his views, and a criticism of them, appear in the chronological survey below.

Mr. Desmond MacCarthy has printed in *The Listener* for 11th December, 1929, a sketch of Watson broadcast a week previously. The limits thus imposed on the length of the narrative prohibited Mr. MacCarthy from dealing in any full manner with Watson, and he does not attempt Holmes. There are some useful points made, however, and we could wish it had been expanded. As it is, it is necessarily eclipsed by the standard work on Dr. Watson,[1] recently given to us by Mr. S. C. Roberts.

In this book, Mr. Roberts has achieved for Watson what he and other scholars have accomplished for Boswell. As the latter now stands rehabilitated from the servile and contemptible figure of a Macauleian legend, so has the character of Watson been lifted by Mr. Roberts above the customary

[1] *Dr. Watson* (Faber & Faber).

picture of him as a slow-witted Victorian whose thick-headedness would be marked even without the brilliant contrast of Holmes's intellect. Since we are concerned here primarily with Holmes, it would be outside our sphere to pass Mr. Roberts's work in detailed review. Suffice it to say that Watson appears as a man of quiet, reliable courage, essentially a man of action and a lover of the adventurous ; devoted to the attractions of gambling ; a chivalrous admirer of women ; a worthy husband and a loyal friend—justifying the claim accorded to him by Mr. MacCarthy as being 'the most representative Englishman of the latter end of the nineteenth century'. No work on the Holmes-Watson association reaches a higher level as literature, and if on such important details as the date of Watson's first marriage, or the identity of his second wife, we are obliged to differ from Mr. Roberts's conclusions, such differences in no way detract from our admiration for this excellent piece of work.

THE CAREER OF SHERLOCK HOLMES

CHRONOLOGICAL SURVEY

As we have already seen,[1] it appears that Holmes came to live in London about 1874. Prior to this he had only handled one mystery, the *Gloria Scott* affair. The date of this important case—important for being the motive cause of Holmes becoming a detective—is therefore about 1873, and it will at once be seen that this does not agree with the details given in the record itself. According to old Trevor, he was convicted in 1855, when the Crimean War was at its height. Both he and Hudson [2] place the occasion thirty years before the sinister reappearance of the latter at Donnithorpe, so the date of this incident should be 1885. This, in view of what we know of Holmes's career, is impossible. We cannot right the difficulty by reading ' twenty ' for ' thirty ' years ago, as it would mean old Trevor married far too late for his son to be a contemporary of Holmes. The only line of escape would seem to be to read 1855 as 1845, and to take the phrase ' thirty years ago ' as just a round figure,

---

[1] See p. 3 above. [2] Hudson says thirty years ' or more '.

twenty-eight being more precise. But then what becomes of the reference to the Crimean War, and the reasons Trevor gives for the Government of the day using the *Gloria Scott* as a convict ship— owing to all the customary ships having been taken up for war work? It is a difficult point, but clearly we cannot abide by the year 1885. We have seen that 1878 is the first year of Holmes's career before the public,[1] and the *Gloria Scott* case cannot have been *less* than four years previous to *The Musgrave Ritual*,[2] which was the third affair Holmes handled after adopting his profession.

Beyond these two cases, we know little enough of Holmes's life prior to the advent of Watson in 1881. At the outset, he tells us, he had a hard struggle to make any headway, and filled in his abundant leisure in acquiring that wide knowledge on all subjects likely to help his work that is so striking in his later years. College friends brought him a few cases, and we must surmise that he had small private means to enable him to live. Like many a striving barrister, he occupied some of his spare time in writing technical works—those famous monographs on tobacco-ash, tracing of footsteps, etc., etc. By degrees, however, a considerable,

---

[1] See p. 3 above.

[2] It was more probably five years earlier, as we have no reason to think Holmes was leaving college at the time, whereas *The Musgrave Ritual* was four years after he and Musgrave had known one another at college.

though not very lucrative practice was built up. Among his cases were the affair of Mrs. Farintosh (a friend of Miss Stoner, later known to us in *The Speckled Band*) ; the Tarleton murders ; the case of Vamberry, the wine merchant ; the adventure of the old Russian woman ; the affair of the aluminium crutch, and the case of Ricoletti of the club-foot and his abominable wife.[1] During these years, when he was laying the foundations of his reputation, he charged fees for consultations,[2] though later he was usually content to work for love. Not all his early cases were successful, and it is possibly during this time that the three occasions when he was beaten by men [3] occurred.[4]

We do not know for certain where he was living when Watson met him first, but perhaps still in Montague Street. He had been for some little time on the look out for larger accommodation, but his means would not run to the Baker Street suite by himself.[5] The Holmes-Watson menage is

---

[1] *The Musgrave Ritual.* [2] *A Study in Scarlet.* [3] *The Five Orange Pips.*
[4] In this connection we may ask whether he can be said to have succeeded in *The Greek Interpreter* and *The Engineer's Thumb*, whilst *The Five Orange Pips* involved the death of his client without the murderers being brought to book, though providentially they were drowned at sea. A similar query may perhaps be entered in the case of *The Resident Patient*, where the murderers were also supposedly lost at sea, and Holmes had not arranged for their capture as he had done in *The Five Orange Pips*.
[5] Mr. Roberts, *Dr. Watson*, p. 14, note 2, accepts Dr. Briggs's deduction that 221B Baker Street was really No. 111. But this is

too well known to all to need any recounting here. Watson had a bull-pup at the time he met Holmes, but whether he was able to keep it at 221B is doubtful. We never hear of it again, and possibly the landlady did not permit pet animals, though she herself kept a dog which died in dramatic circumstances during the investigation of *A Study in Scarlet*. Probably Watson decided not to keep his animal, seeing that he himself could only go out when the weather was favourable—hard treatment for any dog.

Between 1881 and 1887 we have little certain information about Holmes's activities. *The Speckled Band* was in April 1883, and has perhaps achieved a greater notoriety than any other of his cases. It is probably during this period that there took place the investigations of *Silver Blaze*, *The Yellow Face*, *The Greek Interpreter* and *The Beryl Coronet*. The business of *The Red Circle* may also be in these years, for in it we find Inspector Gregson, whom we first meet in *A Study in Scarlet*, but so seldom see in late years that an early date may be assumed for most of his cases. In the year previous to *The Red Circle*, Holmes had arranged an affair for a

certainly wrong. From the directions given us in *The Empty House* —into Manchester Street and so to Blandford Street, then down a side passage—the latter must be either Blandford or Kendall Mews. Camden House was opposite 221B, and the latter would therefore be amongst 45/51 or 29/35. Reliable local authority has informed us that No. 49 is accepted in that district as being upon the site.

Mr. Fairdale Hobbs—evidently a matter of no consequence. In the adventure of *The Yellow Face* we have some indication of the date, for Holmes was at that time only occasionally using cocaine, whereas at the commencement of *The Sign of Four* some years later he had developed the habit badly. Somewhere during this period the incident of *The Resident Patient* took place ; the Worthingdon bank gang got fifteen years in 1875, but came out before their full term. The adventure opened in the month of October, and either of the years 1886 or 1887 seems equally probable. The Bishopgate jewel mystery occurred about 1886/7, when Holmes took the opportunity to lecture Scotland Yard severely on the art of detection.[1]

The case of *Silver Blaze* was, no doubt, recorded by Watson because of his own keen interest in racing,[2] though it is curious that he says nothing of making any bets on the Wessex Cup, whereas we learn that Holmes won on the race. The care of racing was at that time less exact than now[3] ; it would not be possible to-day to run a horse in disguise—Colonel Ross, the owner, it will be remembered, failed even to recognize Silver Blaze. It has been contended that of the people concerned in running the horse, about half should

---

[1] *The Sign of Four.*   [2] *Shoscombe Old Place.*
[3] See *The Times*, 28th March, 1932 : ' Fifty Years : Contrasts on the Turf '.

have gone to gaol, and the rest warned off the turf for ever.[1]

The Greek Interpreter is an important case for students of Sherlock Holmes, for in it we learn something of his family and are first introduced to Mycroft. The grounds for placing it in these early days are to be found in some remarks in *The Bruce-Partington Plans* (1895), when Watson had only a vague recollection of Mycroft at the time of *The Greek Interpreter*. We may fairly conclude from this that the case was a good many years back, and is evidently prior to Watson's first marriage. Holmes also admits that he did not know Watson sufficiently well at the time to feel justified in informing him of the true nature of Mycroft's government post.

According to Holmes himself, it was in 1884 that he boxed with McMurdo on the latter's benefit night at ' the fancy '. It is a little difficult to accept this date, however, for if McMurdo joined Major Sholto's household as one of his two pugilist protectors, it must have been earlier than 1882, the year of Sholto's death. Bartholomew Sholto would hardly have engaged him, as he had no need for a protector, though naturally he would take over his

---

[1] *Memories and Adventures*, by A. C. Doyle, p. 127 *seq.* A writer in the *Strand Magazine*, vol. 53 (1917), p. 58, has claimed the case of *Silver Blaze* as the finest exhibition of Holmes's powers—a view that seems scarcely justified.

father's servants, which accounts for McMurdo's presence at Pondicherry Lodge in 1888. The latter's benefit night (presumably when he retired from the ring) would have been just prior to his being engaged by Major Sholto on the latter's retirement from the Army—about 1877.

In 1887, however, we get back to definite dating. Bert Stevens, the mild-mannered young murderer, was hanged this year,[1] but evidently Holmes's great feat was his handling of the case of the Netherland-Sumatra Company and the schemes of Baron Maupertuis. This was in the spring, probably about February/March, and took place on the Continent. Overwork in the undertaking (Holmes succeeded where the police of three countries had failed) brought about a nervous breakdown, necessitating his convalescing at Reigate in April. The rest-cure, however, was disturbed by the murder near by, with the eventual unmasking of the Cunninghams, father and son. Still, the change did him good, and he returned to London soon after in restored health.

We are told,[2] however, that he had many cases between 1882 and 1890, and we are given the following names for 1887 alone : The Adventures of the Paradol Chamber, the Amateur Mendicant Society, the loss of the barque *Sophy Anderson*, the Grice Patersons in the island of Uffa, and the

---

[1] *The Norwood Builder.*　　　　[2] *The Five Orange Pips.*

Camberwell poisoning case. This latter was evidently one of Holmes's best pieces of work, and Watson's failure to write it up fully is much to be regretted.

With the year 1888 we come to the most difficult chronological problem in the history of Holmes and Watson, which is the latter's marriage and its time-relation to various cases known to us. This problem has never yet been dealt with fully, not even by Mr. Roberts, and it is time, therefore, that the data be thoroughly reviewed.

Since Watson became engaged to Miss Morstan after their meeting during the investigation of *The Sign of Four*, we are primarily concerned with the date of this case.

As we all know, the traditional opening was on 7th July, 1888.[1] But against the acceptance of this date there have been brought a number of arguments, based mainly upon the dates attributed to other cases.

(1) *The Reigate Squires*, April 1887, is before Watson's marriage.

[1] Mr. Roberts, *Dr. Watson*, p. 16, dates *The Sign of Four* to April/June, which clashes with the postmark on Thaddeus Sholto's letter. Mr. MacCarthy, *The Listener*, 11th December, 1929, dates the adventure on the day following, 8th July, but has overlooked the fact that the letter speaks of Miss Morstan being required to go to the Lyceum 'to-night', and she received it that very morning. Clearly the letter was not written till after midnight on the 6th, and would not therefore catch the first delivery on the 7th; hence Miss Morstan did not call on Holmes till after lunch.

(2) *The Five Orange Pips*, September 1887, occurred after the marriage.

(3) *A Scandal in Bohemia*, March 1888, is still later, and supports the contention that *The Five Orange Pips* was shortly after the wedding. By March '88 Watson and Holmes had drifted apart, and the latter had been far afield—to Holland and Odessa. Watson had put on seven pounds in weight since his wedding—a sure indication of a lapse of time.

(4) An ingenious argument, due to Mr. Desmond MacCarthy, is that since Miss Morstan had received a large pearl every 4th May commencing in 1882, by July 1888 she should have exhibited seven pearls, not the six noted by Watson.

(5) *The Noble Bachelor* took place within a few weeks of Watson's marriage, and from internal evidence is in October, 1887.

From points (4) and (5) Mr. MacCarthy concludes that *The Sign of Four* is in July 1887, and Watson's wedding in the late autumn of the same year. This appears also to be the view of Mr. R. I. Gunn, as quoted by Mr. Roberts.[1]

Mr. Roberts himself prefers to place the marriage between April and September, 1887, relying on points (1) and (2). *The Sign of Four* he throws

[1] *Dr. Watson*, p. 18, note 2.

back to 1886. Thus we see that the arguments against the traditional date of the latter case do not furnish us with precise information, but, on the contrary, give us two separate and equally plausible sets of data both for *The Sign of Four* and the year of Watson's marriage. This is scarcely an encouraging commencement.

Turning now to the assignment of *The Sign of Four* to the year 1888, we find this rests upon a good deal of very consistent data :—

(*a*) Captain Morstan came home in 1878, when his daughter was seventeen, and Watson observes that in that case 'she must be seven-and-twenty now'. This gives us the year 1888.

(*b*) Miss Morstan gives the exact date of her father's disappearance—3rd December, 1878—'nearly ten years ago'.

(*c*) She also says Major Sholto 'had retired some little time before' her father's death, which Thaddeus Sholto corroborates by saying his father 'retired some eleven years ago'

(*d*) The advertisement for Miss Morstan appeared 'about six years ago—to be exact, upon the 4th of May, 1882'.

(*e*) Holmes, turning up the back files of *The Times*, found that Major Sholto died upon the 28th April, 1882, which he notes was within a week of Miss Morstan receiving her first pearl. This corroborates point (*d*).

(*f*) Holmes further observes that Sholto's death (*vide* ' *The Times* ') was four years after Morstan's, so we have corroboration of point (*b*).

(*g*) Thaddeus Sholto says that early in 1882 his father received a letter from India, and ' towards the end of April ' he died. This is further evidence (though none is needed) of Sholto's date of decease.

(*h*) Watson remarks that it is odd Sholto's heir should ' write a letter now, rather than six years ago ', and as Sholto's date of death cannot be in doubt, we again reach 1888 as the current year. Should it be said that Watson erred in using the word ' six ', we may compare Holmes's observation that the Sholtos were six years searching for the treasure.

(*i*) Jonathan Small did ' twenty long years ' in the Andaman Islands. The relief of Agra by Greathed was, as a matter of history, on 10th October, 1857, and as the Mutiny was virtually over before Small was arrested, his trial was certainly not earlier than 1858. He was in prison first in Agra, then Madras, before he proceeded to the Andamans, where he would arrive about

1860. Add his twenty years, plus the considerable time on his journey to England (as described), plus the time taken in locating Major Sholto, and we can see that the spring of 1882 as the date of the latter's death is just about right.[1]

(*j*) In *The Veiled Lodger* we are told that Watson was with Holmes for seventeen years. He married a second time at the end of 1902 or very early 1903. From 1894 [2] to 1902, both years inclusive, gives nine of the seventeen years, so the remaining eight are from 1881 [3] to 1888. Since *The Sign of Four* must have been *one* of the last cases in which Watson was associated with Holmes prior to his first marriage, 1888 seems the proper year for it.

We thus see that the internal evidence checks itself very well ; indeed, *The Sign of Four* is more amply authenticated than any other case of Sherlock Holmes. Only the strongest proof of its inaccuracy can overthrow the dating of 1888, and such proof, we contend, is lacking.

Much has been made of the dates given to *A Scandal in Bohemia* and *The Five Orange Pips*. As

[1] It is true, Small speaks of arriving in England ' some three or four years ago ', but he is not attempting chronological accuracy.

[2] The year of ' The Return '.

[3] *A Study in Scarlet*.

regards the latter, it is clear that it must be *later*, not earlier, than *A Scandal in Bohemia*, as conclusively proved by Holmes's remark to Openshaw that he had been beaten four times, three times by men and once by a woman. The latter is unquestionably Irene Adler.

Mr. Roberts lays great stress [1] on ' the extremely precise ' dating of *A Scandal in Bohemia*, viz. 20th March, 1888. But if we look more closely into the matter, the date becomes a little less precise. The betrothal of the King of Bohemia was to be announced on the following Monday, and Holmes remarked that there were three days in which to act. If we exclude the Sunday from the ' working ' days, these three days of action would be Thursday, Friday and Saturday. The interview, therefore, of the King with Holmes was on the Wednesday (this day was not included in the days of action, as the King did not call till the evening). Now the almanac tells us that the 20th March, 1889, *was* a Wednesday, but in 1888 a Tuesday. The precise dating is exact enough if the year 1889 is chosen, and as we shall see, this is what is required by other cases.

The Engineer's Thumb, in the summer of 1889, was ' not long after my marriage '. This seems a reasonable enough description, if the marriage was towards the close of 1888, as we believe, but quite

[1] *Dr. Watson*, p. 17. (See also his *Note on the Watson Problem*, p. 5.)

inaccurate if the year was 1887. Had it been the latter, we might expect Watson to write that *The Engineer's Thumb* was in the second year of his married life (as, for example, he does in *The Dying Detective*).

The Crooked Man was ' a few months after' Watson's marriage. The garrison at Bhurtee was relieved by Neill's column, and this column we know from history was operating from May to September 1857 (Neill was killed at Lucknow 25th September).[1] Barclay may have married in 1857, but more likely in '58, when things had quieted down in India. Holmes says that at the time of his death Barclay had been married for ' upwards of thirty years ', and this is checked by Mrs. Barclay's remark to Wood, that he was thought to have been dead ' this thirty years '. Add over thirty years to 1858, and we may fairly reach 1889, the more so as this case, occurring in the summer, must have been much the same time as *The Engineer's Thumb*, which is expressly declared to be in 1889.

The Boscombe Valley Mystery, where Watson, judging by his breakfast-table remark to his wife, seems newly married, is about the same date. John Turner was a bandit in the early sixties, had turned over a new leaf, come to England, and was com-

[1] See J. W. Fortescue, *History of the British Army*, xiii, pp. 263 *seq.*, 314.

fortably settled—all covering some years—before
he again met McCarthy, who had had a grip on
him ' these twenty years ',[1] bringing us once more
to about 1889.

The Cardboard Box is later than *The Sign of Four*,
in the month of August, and Watson appears to be
unmarried. It was some while after Gordon's
death (January 1885), but not so very long after
Beecher's (March 1887), for the former's picture
was framed, but the latter's not. We would place
it in August 1888, since we learn elsewhere that
there was an abundance of cases for the year 1887,[2]
which would leave little time available to fit *The
Cardboard Box* into the same year.

A Case of Identity, we learn, is later than *A Scandal
in Bohemia*, but not much, for though it is only a
few weeks since Holmes last saw Watson, the latter
had not seen the King of Bohemia's present. On
the other hand, the *Case of Identity* is earlier than
The Man with the Twisted Lip (June 1889). Since
we learn from *The Blue Carbuncle* (which, like
Mr. Roberts [3] and Fr. Knox,[4] we date Christmas
1889) that *A Scandal in Bohemia*, *A Case of Identity*
and *The Man with the Twisted Lip* are three of the
last six cases added to Watson's notes, they must
all fall in the same year, viz. 1889—1888 is im-

[1] A vague period, probably indicative of more than twenty years.
[2] See above, p. 53.   [3] *Dr. Watson*, p. 23.
[4] *Essays in Satire*, p. 156.

possible for them all. The point seems clinched by *The Engineer's Thumb*, which, as already seen, was in the summer of '89, 'not long after my marriage'.

Briefly, in our view three alterations have to be made. *The Noble Bachelor* is 1888, and *A Scandal in Bohemia* 1889. These alterations throw nothing else out of gear ; so far, indeed, is this from being the case with the latter adventure, that we have seen that the change brings it into line with *A Case of Identity*, *The Man with the Twisted Lip* and *The Blue Carbuncle*. The third alteration is more serious —*The Five Orange Pips*. This would need to be thrown forward two years—to 1889. This clashes with Openshaw's remark that his father died in January 1885, 'and two years and eight months have elapsed since then ', as well as with Watson's dating. In justification, we must point out that *The Five Orange Pips* falls foul of something in whatever year it is placed. We have seen that it must be later than the Irene Adler affair, and we may add that if it is put forward to 1889, we find it shortly before *The Hound of the Baskervilles*, and obtain for the latter an explanation of Watson's living at Baker Street, and not with his wife, whose visit to her aunt (*vide* ' *The Five Orange Pips* ') may easily have been prolonged into October.

Mr. Desmond MacCarthy's dating of *The Sign of Four* to July 1887 explains, as intended, the six

pearls [1] instead of seven, but clashes with every
other date in the record. The traditional dates for
The Noble Bachelor and *A Scandal in Bohemia*, it is
true, fit in with 1887, but *The Five Orange Pips* would
need to be put forward one year at least ; neither
The Engineer's Thumb nor *The Man with the Twisted
Lip* will fit, and great difficulties arise with *The
Resident Patient*, *The Cardboard Box* and *The Crooked
Man*. The required correlation of *A Scandal in
Bohemia*, *A Case of Identity*, *The Man with the Twisted
Lip* and *The Blue Carbuncle* is set at naught.

Mr. Roberts's arrangement squares *The Five
Orange Pips* with *A Scandal in Bohemia*, though
Holmes's opening remarks in the latter case do not
fit in very well. If he had had Watson staying with
him six months earlier, he would surely have
learned of the latter's intention to return to practice.
Nor do Watson's remarks in *The Stockbroker's Clerk*,
that he had not seen much of Holmes since his
marriage, accord very well with his having stayed
with him within three months of marrying (apart
from the improbability of a newly-married man
doing any such thing). But we are compelled to
say that the dating of *The Sign of Four* to 1886

[1] This difficulty is not insuperable. Miss Morstan may have had
the first pearl she received made up into a brooch or pendant, as
she would not be expecting any more ; but naturally, on finding
pearls came in every year, she would keep the remaining six together.
Again, Watson may have counted wrong—see Mr. Roberts's remarks
on his state of mind (op. cit., p. 17).

makes even worse havoc of the other dates in the record than Mr. MacCarthy's preference for 1887. *The Noble Bachelor* does not agree with Mr. Roberts's dating, and if, at a pinch, *The Boscombe Valley Mystery* might be made to do so, *The Engineer's Thumb* is right out of it. We have grave doubts of bringing *The Resident Patient, The Crooked Man* or *The Cardboard Box* into line, and again, there is no correlation of *A Scandal in Bohemia, A Case of Identity, The Man with the Twisted Lip* and *The Blue Carbuncle*.

We conclude, therefore, that *The Sign of Four* took place in July 1888, and Watson's marriage towards the close of that year—probably November. The internal evidence of *The Sign of Four* calls for the year 1888 : an abundance of other evidence substantiates it. The maintenance of this date requires less alteration elsewhere than any other arrangement, and, if the conclusion cannot be proved with apodeictic certainty, we venture to think we have made it extremely probable.

If, then, we are driven to believe in the authenticity of 1888 as the year of *The Sign of Four*, the arrangement of Holmes's recorded cases would seem to be :—

July—*The Sign of Four*.
August—*The Cardboard Box*.
September—The King of Scandinavia's affairs.
October—*The Noble Bachelor*.
In November (possibly December) came Watson's

marriage. Mr. Roberts suggests that Holmes would hardly be best man, or Watson would have recorded the fact. Since, however, Watson never even records his wedding, he could hardly mention what part in it Holmes may have played. On one other occasion we find Holmes as best man—in Irene Adler's wedding.

Any regrets which Holmes may have felt at the parting with Watson (and we may, on evidence elsewhere given us, believe that he entertained them) were, no doubt, quickly swallowed up in the exigencies of his work. He had soon to handle a delicate matter for the royal house of Holland [1]—a case so intimate that he could not relate it even to Watson [2]; a visit was paid to Odessa in connection with the Trepoff murder; and the tragedy of the Atkinson brothers at Trincomalee involved his attention. [1] There is no evidence that Holmes had to go to Ceylon for the latter case, and we know he avoided long absences if possible, owing to the unhealthy activity shown during such periods by the London criminal world. [3] Four months thus went by before Watson next came into touch with Holmes, on the very evening of the visit of the King of Bohemia. [4]

---

[1] *A Scandal in Bohemia.*   [2] *A Case of Identity.*

[3] *Lady Frances Carfax* (cp. also *The Cardboard Box* and *The Hound of the Baskervilles*).

[4] It was not difficult for Holmes to identify his visitor as the king, once he had located Bohemia as the country of residence, for the royal ' we ' had crept into the letter of appointment.

The early part of 1889 found Holmes a very busy
man, but his recorded cases are not numerous.
The Irene Adler matter was soon over, and the
Case of Identity, which followed a few weeks later—
April or May—did not necessitate any great labour
for Holmes, who realized the true explanation even
as Miss Sutherland told her story. ' There was
never such a person ' (as Mr. Hosmer Angel), he
told her when she took her leave, and most of us,
no doubt, could wish he had got in a few lashes
with his dogwhip before Mr. Windigate ran from
the house. At the time of this incident Holmes had
about a dozen cases on hand, but only one (a continental inquiry) was of any special interest. The
Dundas separation case, in which he had been
consulted, was just over, and this, together with
the other twelve cases, afford us evidence that,
apart from the problems put on record by Watson,
Holmes handled a multitude of small fry, of which
we hear little or nothing. One or two are referred
to by Watson in *A Study in Scarlet*, no doubt striking
his attention more forcibly then, when he was still
a stranger to Holmes's profession. Mrs. Forrester [1]
and Major Prendergast [2] are other instances, and
on a few occasions the stories of these trivialities of
his work are told to us. [3]

We learn in *A Case of Identity* that Holmes had

[1] *The Sign of Four.*   [2] *The Five Orange Pips.*
[3] *The Veiled Lodger, The Yellow Face,* and *A Case of Identity* itself.

overcome the evident dislike he entertained for the King of Bohemia during the Irene Adler investigation, and had accepted a present from him, though at the time he had coldly refused the King's offer. Perhaps a little sense of pique had governed his first refusal, although in the case of Thor Bridge, his rebuke (if accurately recorded) to Neil Gibson on the subject of the latter's attention to Miss Dunbar, shows that, as with the King of Bohemia, Holmes was very sensitive to unchivalrous behaviour towards women. He himself was always a chivalrous opponent, Watson remarks, though he disliked and distrusted the sex.

The summer of 1889 proved a busy time for both Holmes and Watson, and the latter collaborated with his old friend in a number of cases. So much was this the case, indeed, that it is difficult not to surmise that his practice was at best only occasionally busy, for his absences with Holmes were sometimes prolonged. It must be remembered, of course, that Watson's predecessor, Mr. Farquhar, had let the business go down badly, so lack of work was probably no fault of his own. His immediate neighbour was a rival in his profession, and had, no doubt, made hay during the sunshine of Mr. Farquhar's misfortunes. Watson probably bought the practice about February/March, as at the time of *A Scandal in Bohemia*, Holmes did not know he had returned to his old profession. He did not buy it till after his marriage, as he tells us in *The Stockbroker's Clerk*, at which time (early June 1889) he had been hard at work for some three months.

Holmes was occupied with the investigation (at the Pope's request) of the affair of the Vatican cameos during June '89,[1] but we do not know over how long a period this was spread. *The Stockbroker's Clerk* is apparently the first case during June, and occurred on a Saturday. It reads as if it was the first meeting of Holmes and Watson for some time, so should fall prior to *The Boscombe Valley Mystery*, where the murder took place on 3rd June. If so, Saturday, the 1st June, should be the date for the former case, but it is possible to adopt the 15th, as Holmes speaks of the wet June they had been having, which suggests a later date than the first of the month. But we incline to the 1st June, and it is noticeable that though Watson had visited Holmes two or three times since his marriage, Holmes had never come to see him till now. Hence his first inquiries are after Mrs. Watson, and he finds grounds for a few deductions as to the relative values of Watson's and his neighbour's practices. Watson was able at a moment's notice to go to Birmingham with Holmes, but as the day was a Saturday, he was probably less busy than usual. The case was soon over, but neither

[1] *The Hound of the Baskervilles.*

was left long in peace, for the next week they were summoned to go down to Boscombe. The day of the visit was probably Thursday or Friday, for Holmes speaks of the crime having occurred on ' Monday last ', so if they had been going down less than three days after, he would have said ' yesterday ' or ' the day before yesterday '. They stayed one night, and returned to town with the satisfaction of having solved the mystery. The strange business of *The Man with the Twisted Lip* soon followed, but in this case Holmes, no doubt recollecting his two recent intrusions into the Watson menage, did not call on his friend to join him till accident brought them together in the opium den in Upper Swandam Lane. The day we know was a Friday, for Watson was at pains to impress the fact upon Isa Whitney, but the date is wrongly given, as 19th June this year fell on a Wednesday. Evidently Watson has carelessly written down the date of Whitney's disappearance, whereas he should have recorded the 21st. Neville St. Clair was unmasked the following day, when Watson, no doubt, returned home.

In July he approached Holmes to gain his aid on behalf of the unhappy ' Tadpole ' Phelps in the matter of *The Naval Treaty*. Holmes had a number of other cases on hand, and was engaged upon a chemical analysis bearing upon a murder when Watson came upon him. It would be interesting to know whether Joseph Harrison was caught ; what the Inspector, who had hardly welcomed Holmes at the outset, had to say when he found that Joseph had fled, though virtually arrested by Holmes, we would also like to learn. It is noticeable how the latter still looked to Watson to assist him, if required, regardless of the other's work. What he misconceived to be a hint from his friend that he must return to his practice was treated with scant courtesy.

The Adventure of the Tired Captain was contemporary with *The Naval Treaty*, but Watson never wrote it up.

Both *The Engineer's Thumb* (one of the few cases introduced to Holmes by Watson) and *The Crooked Man* occurred in the summer of 1889, but precise dates are not given. Presumably, however, as we have seen that June was well occupied, these cases could hardly have been during that month, as Watson could never have spared so much time from his profession. July to August seems more likely. The importance of these cases, as evidence for the date of Watson's marriage, has already been noted. *The Abbas Parva* affair [1] probably occurred about the same time as *The Five Orange Pips*—viz. September 1889—as Watson was living with Holmes at the time of the former, and we know he had returned to Baker Street prior to John Openshaw's

[1] *The Veiled Lodger.*

visit. As already noted, it seems certain that Mrs. Watson's visit to her aunt was prolonged for some while beyond the few days originally intended, for *The Five Orange Pips* is during the latter days of September, and *The Hound of the Baskervilles* early October.[1] Watson's cheerful absence from his practice is surely proof that it was not a hard-worked one—no doubt the obliging Anstruther[2] was able to cope with whatever it entailed. At the time of this case Holmes had a blackmailing affair in hand, and after the close of ' The Hound ' he handled the card scandal at the Nonpareil Club, and was also successful in acquitting Mme Montpensier of the unfounded charge of murdering her stepdaughter, whose reappearance later on in America proved the justness of the defence. He rightly recognized, however, in the persecutor of the Baskervilles a foeman worthy of his every effort, and accordingly went down also to Dartmoor—but not with Watson. Although the case did not involve any feats of detection for Holmes, there is

[1] Sir Henry Baskerville's party travelled down to Dartmoor on a Saturday, and the Saturdays in October 1889 fell on 5th, 12th, etc. Watson's first report was dated the 13th, and before then he had sent Holmes telegrams and letters. The journey down was therefore probably on the 5th October, and certainly not later. The date of Dr. Mortimer's first call on Holmes would be approximately 1st October.

[2] Jackson was Watson's next-door neighbour, to judge from his remarks in *The Crooked Man* and *The Stockbroker's Clerk*. Anstruther, perhaps, was his assistant for a while.

none more dramatic than his silent contest with Stapleton and the eventual laying of the family ghost in the body of the terrible hound. We have a side-light on the greater self-control possessed by both Holmes and Watson than by Lestrade, who was quite unnerved by the appearance of the hound, whilst the others had the presence of mind to fire at the beast. Nowhere, perhaps, do we find better evidence of Holmes's nerve and courage than in this case ; to dwell alone on the moor, in a comfortless stone hut, would be an ' eerie ' business at the best of times ; with the knowledge of the hound's existence near at hand, and the uses for which it might at any night be let loose—to say nothing of the presence of the murderer Selden —would call for no common gifts of fearlessness.

Watson and Holmes probably returned to London before the end of October, and the former no doubt got back to his sadly-neglected duties. Beyond the fact of his visiting Baker Street to hear the details of Stapleton's life from Holmes, we hear no more till after Christmas, when the doctor opportunely called at 221B on the day that the Countess of Morcar's blue carbuncle came to light in the crop of a Christmas goose. The opening pages of this record are among the most attractive we possess, and rank with the commencement of *The Valley of Fear*, *The Sign of Four*, and *The Hound of the Baskervilles* as exhibitions of Holmes's powers of reasoning.

At the outset of 1890 we come to a point of certain chronological difficulty. In our view, we must attribute to January of this year *The Valley of Fear.*
Our data for this case are as follows :—

(1) We are told it was on January 7 that Holmes received Porlock's letter, and the death at Birlstone was on the night previous. (Watson speaks of the year being ' at the end of the eighties '.)

(2) John Douglas took over the Manor House of Birlstone five years previously, and Cecil Barker told the detectives it was nearer seven than six years before the affair that Douglas had left California.

(3) The narrative of the Scowrers opens on February 4, 1875, when Birdie Edwards arrived at Vermissa, and he was there for some three months. The rounding up of McGinty and his associates would therefore be some time in May 1875. Ted Baldwin, the only one who really concerns us, got ten years' imprisonment, so was out in 1885.

(4) Douglas's departure from California coincided with Baldwin and some others getting on his trail. No doubt the Scowrers had had agents outside prison

to keep Douglas traced, so presumably
they were not long in travelling to
Benito Canyon after the conclusion of the
ten years in prison.

(5) On the face of it, it would seem that
Douglas left California in 1885, which
was about seven years previous to the
killing of Baldwin at Birlstone. The
latter event, therefore, would appear to
take place on January 6, 1892.

The objection, of course, to this is (apart from
Watson's statement of the year, which is too vague
to be more than a very rough guide), that by 1892
Holmes was believed dead (though actually travelling in Tibet) and Professor Moriarty had quite
certainly departed this life. Yet according to *The
Valley of Fear* the professor was then very much alive,
and the duel between him and Holmes was at
most in its initial stages. Watson, it may be noted,
is living at Baker Street, and admits to some knowledge of Moriarty. Yet on the 24th April, 1891,
he told Holmes he had never heard the name, and
Moriarty reminded him during his interview that
their paths had crossed for the first time on
January 4 of that year. It is tempting to try and
identify this latter date with *The Valley of Fear*, but
the objections to so doing are considerable.
Moriarty's phrase, ' crossed my path ', must be
taken to mean that Holmes had in some degree,

not perhaps very large, *hampered* the professor's
activities, but he cannot be said to have done so
in *The Valley of Fear*, since Douglas was ' removed '
quite satisfactorily some little time later. Moriarty
was bound to know of Holmes, as did most London
criminals, long before the clash came, and on the
latter's own showing in *The Valley of Fear* he knew
all about Moriarty, and had warned Scotland Yard
accordingly. What seems most plausible is that
Holmes worked quietly and waited patiently for
many months—more than a year, in fact—before
he was in a position to start his contest with
Moriarty, on 4th January, 1891. *The Valley of
Fear*, therefore, would have to go back to an earlier
year than '91 (to say nothing of '92), yet surely
cannot be before 1890, since January 1889 was
only a few weeks after Watson's wedding, and,
however frequently Mrs. Watson may have visited
her aunt and Watson rejoined Holmes in later times,
can we believe they would do so so early in their
married life ? To go back earlier than 1889 would
leave too long a gap altogether between the time
of Holmes's early knowledge of Moriarty and his
bringing him to book. The justification for the
date of January 1890 (and indeed *any* date other
than 1892, which is itself impossible) requires that
Baldwin got out before his full term of ten years,
and there is nothing unlikely about that. If such
a murderous villain could escape the death

penalty, there would be nothing improbable in his managing to get out of prison before his time, whether by good conduct or by bribery. The latter course seems most likely, since the police in America were evidently no less corrupt then than now.[1]

To explain Watson's profession of ignorance of the name of Moriarty in *The Final Problem* is more difficult. He wrote the account in 1893, and his recollections may have become somewhat disturbed or vague.[2] As his object in writing it was to rebut Colonel Moriarty's attempted rehabilitation of his brother's character, it was perhaps natural, though hardly excusable, in Watson to concentrate on the facts of *The Final Problem* to the exclusion of other cases, such as *The Valley of Fear*, with which Professor Moriarty had a less definite association. Moreover, it was probably during 1893 that Mrs. Watson died,[3] after prolonged ill-health, an additional cir-

---

[1] See part ii of *The Valley of Fear* for examples of the influence of the Scowrers on the course of justice and in prison affairs.

[2] He had not a specially good memory : he had only vague recollections in 1895 of Mycroft Holmes, whose mode of life he had so much forgotten as to cause him no surprise at the latter visiting Baker Street, whereas it was as unusual as meeting a tram in a country lane (see *The Bruce-Partington Plans*) ; at the time of *The Veiled Lodger* (1896) he had forgotten the *Abbas Parva* case, only seven years before.

[3] S. C. Roberts, *Dr. Watson*, pp. 23, 24. Mrs. Watson probably died of heart-trouble, inherited from her father. Twice in *The Sign of Four* she turned faint on very slight provocation.

cumstance which would tend to throw Watson out of gear. In any event, unless we can detect an editorial adumbration,[1] either Watson's profession of knowledge of Moriarty in *The Valley of Fear* or his ignorance in *The Final Problem* must be regarded (and deplored) as a piece of literary licence to give artistic verisimilitude to his narrative. The probability, perhaps, is that an editorial hand has touched up (not very successfully) *The Valley of Fear*, for we find Watson saying that ' a long series of sterile weeks ' lay behind this adventure, which is clearly untrue, as *The Blue Carbuncle* was less than a fortnight before, and *The Hound of the Baskervilles* had only been rounded off (amidst great pressure of other work) by Holmes at the latter end of November. The reference to the case falling in the late eighties, instead of early nineties, may also be due to an editor.

One of the few other cases in 1890 we know of is *The Red-Headed League*, in October. The inaccuracy with which Watson wrote up this curious affair in the following year [2] is very noticeable, but is perhaps to be explained by the (presumed) death of Holmes shortly before, which evidently hit Watson hard,[3] and which may well have prevented

---

[1] See p. 37 *seq.*, above.
[2] He tells us *The Red-Headed League* was in the autumn of ' last year '.
[3] See the closing sentences of *The Final Problem*.

him from taking proper care to be chronologically
exact. Having told us that he called on Holmes
in the *autumn*, he records the date of the advertisement for red-headed men in the *Morning Chronicle*
as being 27th April, 'just two months ago'!
On the other hand Mr. Jabez Wilson called upon
Holmes on the same day as he found the notice
of the dissolution of the Red-Headed League,
which was 9th October, and, he also tells us,
the advertisement was brought to his notice by
Spaulding 'just this day eight weeks'. Holmes
remarks that 'to-day is a Saturday', which would
be the natural day for Spaulding to choose for his
bank-breaking job, since he would have the week-
end clear for his escape. Such being the case, as
Mr. Wilson was paid his £4 a week every Saturday
morning, he was not paid for the current week's
work. If, then, he had, as Holmes remarked, got
£32 from his job (he himself speaks of the 'joke'
as costing the perpetrators 'over thirty pounds')
the advertisement must have appeared *nine* weeks
before, and not eight; or, in the alternative, he
had only been paid for seven weeks' work, and
had received £28. In view of the specific statement, repeated more than once, that eight weeks
had passed since the appearance of the advertisement, we seem bound to assume that Watson
wrongly recorded the amount of money paid to
Mr. Wilson.

As final evidence of Watson's errancy, it must regretfully be stated that the almanac shows 9th October, 1890, to have been a *Thursday*; the Scotland Yard detective is referred to as ' Peter ' instead of ' Athelney ' Jones : and Holmes is made to speak of the *Case of Identity* as occurring only ' the other day '. Since it was about eighteen months previous, the phrase is hardly applicable. On the other hand, the fact that Holmes could refer to his conversation on that occasion is additional reason for regarding the *Case of Identity* as belonging to 1889, not 1888. It is surprising enough that Holmes and Watson should recall the details of a conversation of the year previous, but it would be scarcely credible that they would do so had it taken place thirty months before.

Clearly, the advertisement in the *Morning Chronicle* was on 16th August, and Mr. Jabez Wilson's visit to Baker Street on 11th October, 1890. Watson had evidently given up his Paddington practice, and betaken himself to Kensington, where he was still situated in 1894.[1]

In November there occurred the graphically-recorded affair of *The Dying Detective*, which witnesses not to Holmes's detective powers but to his capabilities as an actor, and he could with justice speak of his pretence having been ' carried out with the thoroughness of the true artist '.

[1] *The Empty House.*

79

In the spring of 1891 came the momentous event, *The Final Problem*. Watson had not seen Holmes very recently, but had heard occasionally of and from him. The latter had, it seems, only shortly before completed the case he had been handling for the Scandinavian Royal Family since the autumn of 1888,[1] and he had also finished an important undertaking on behalf of the French Government. The rewards he received for these investigations were so handsome that he might have retired from detective work altogether, and devoted his energies to chemistry, but for the presence of Professor Moriarty at large among society. ' I could not rest, Watson,' he says, ' I could not sit quiet in my chair, if I thought that such a man as Professor Moriarty were walking the streets of London unchallenged.' Since the first introduction of Moriarty a year previously, Holmes had patiently been feeling his way towards the sinister figure of the mathematician, and on the 4th of January, 1891, he for the first time crossed the master-criminal's path. Moriarty's standing in the world had altered in the twelve months' interval : dark stories had got into circulation about him, and his university chair had had to be vacated. The loss of the £700 a year it brought him was of no account to a man of his wealth, but the loss in status was considerable, and he had therefore

[1] *The Noble Bachelor.*

set up as an Army coach. The three months of
silent warfare with Holmes had ended with the
latter holding all the strategic positions, and his
elimination was, therefore, imperative. Whether
Moriarty really expected to induce his opponent to
drop the business rather than court death is doubtful, but it seems certain that he gave Holmes the
warning from a genuine sense of admiration for the
ability with which the battle had been conducted.[1]
The dramatic process of events that led to the final
encounter on the precipices of the Reichenbach
Falls occupied less than a fortnight. It is odd that
Holmes did not realize Moriarty was escaping while
the going was good, but thought he was merely
pursuing him and Watson. The Professor's personal freedom was more important to him at the
moment than Holmes's death, for there was only
one day left before the police rounded up his gang.
Holmes missed a master-stroke by not arranging
for Moriarty to be arrested on arrival at the Channel
port, and be kept quietly incarcerated over Sunday
till the sweep up of the London gang had been
effected on the Monday. Colonel Moran, it is
true, would have been left at large, but as he was
in any case (and Holmes had no knowledge of the

---

[1] Holmes for his part was full of admiration for the Professor's
ability : see his remarks at the opening of *The Final Problem*, and
in the note left at the Reichenbach Falls ; cp. also *The Empty House*
and *The Norwood Builder*.

fact till later), no additional harm would have been done. It is likely enough that Moran travelled separately from Moriarty, with a rendezvous on the Continent, as such splitting of forces would lead less easily to detection. It says little for Scotland Yard that, at so critical a time, they could let Moriarty, undisguised, escape out of England, nor does it seem entirely clear why Watson's suggestion, that Moriarty should at once be arrested, should result in the escape of all the small fry. Since Holmes and the police knew all the men, or most of them at least, they could have been kept under supervision over the week-end, and gathered in at the appointed time. Even if a few ' broken fighting-men ' had escaped, what was that compared with the capture of the mainspring of the London criminal-world ? Such men were of no account, with Moriarty's brains taken away from them ; a few [1] indeed did get clear from the trials following the arrest of the gang, but they never did anything, though they had Colonel Moran behind them.

However, escape Moriarty and Moran did, to leave trouble in store for Holmes. Moriarty had agents on the Continent, [2] who no doubt spotted Holmes and Watson in their unhurried journeyings across Europe, and set their principals on the track.

[1] For example, Parker (see *The Empty House*).
[2] The boy from the Meiringen hotel was one.

Moran seems to have kept at a distance, for he was not referred to by the hotel keeper at Meiringen, who had noticed Moriarty only.

The reasons given by Holmes at a later date [1] for his daring ascent of the rock-wall above the Reichenbach are unsatisfactory. If he were believed dead, he affirmed, his enemies in Moriarty's gang would drop their caution, commit indiscretions, and leave themselves open to his attack. But at the time he was excogitating these considerations, he was unaware that any of Moriarty's followers were at large ! On the contrary, he had recently had a wire from the London police saying (not quite accurately, as events were to prove) that they had secured the whole organization. Holmes did not become aware of Colonel Moran's presence till after he had acted upon his idea, and his statement of his thoughts, as given to Watson, must have been coloured by wisdom after the event. No doubt he was content to give Watson a brief excuse for what amounted to an unkind deception of his distracted friend, but the full explanation must be somewhat different. Holmes, we may remember, was no longer tied, nor had been for some while, in any way by Watson's presence as a dwelling companion ; he was at liberty, therefore, to act just as it pleased him. He had, moreover, by the death of Moriarty and the arrest of his

[1] *The Empty House.*

associates, brought to a conclusion the most dangerous investigation he had ever encountered. What
must have been the strain on him, fighting alone
the huge criminal machine, can only be imagined,
but he had certainly earned a holiday. He was,
we may believe, somewhat overwrought at this
time ; the danger of the Moriarty gang had caused
him to be perpetually on the *qui vive*—adopting
disguises, defending himself against footpads, taking
cover from air-guns, having his habitation set on
fire—and to a naturally highly-strung man this
would tell on his nerves. Once before,[1] at least,
he had collapsed after a prolonged and severe investigation ; he might do so again. So he would
get right away, and not return till the whole
Moriarty business had been forgotten, and if the
trial of Moriarty's men should leave any of them
at liberty, or enable others to regain their freedom
in a short time, it would be all the better for him if
they thought him dead. Once he had adopted
the plan, he could hardly go back on it : consequently, when he found that he had been observed
by Moriarty's companion, he was bound to con-
tinue with his scheme (useless though it would be
for the purposes of deceiving his enemies) since
Watson and the search-party had already departed.

Holmes escaped to Florence, and spent the next

[1] *The Reigate Squires.*

two years travelling in Tibet under an assumed name. Possibly he approached that isolated country from some other direction than India, where the chances of being recognized would be greater than elsewhere, and where the obstacles to penetrating into the Forbidden Land were likely to be prohibitive. Perhaps he obtained permission from the Russian authorities to travel through Central Asia, thus anticipating General Waters in his journeyings in Transcaspia and Samarkand three years later,[1] and being the forerunner of Sir Aurel Stein in Chinese Turkestan. We incline to think he may have entered Tibet from the north-west, with Charklik, perhaps, as his starting-point. Had he approached from Kashmir, he would almost certainly have attracted attention, as Captain Bower was then commencing his travels from Ladak to China. Similarly, Mr. Rockhill would surely have heard of Holmes, had the latter approached from the north-east. A journey from Charklik through, say, the Tsaidam basin, skirting the Koko-shili mountains to the east, and thence south to Lhasa, would break new ground, M. Bonvalot having taken a more westerly route to Tengri-nor via the Chi-chang-tso a year or two before. It is likely that Holmes returned via Khotan to Kashgar, and thence via Persia to

[1] See *Secret and Confidential,* by Brig.-General W. H-H. Waters, chap. vii.

85

Arabia, and eventually Khartoum. However that may be, his explorations were ' remarkable ', and being extended over nearly three years, probably covered much fresh ground. On the return journey he ' looked in at Mecca ', but we are not told in what guise he succeeded in reaching the Sacred City. He must have obtained a working knowledge, to put it at its lowest, of Arabic for this venture, but we must presume that he conversed with the Dalai Lama at Lhasa by means of an interpreter.[1] He put in some time at Montpelier in France, in chemical research, before returning to London, to which he hastened back on hearing of the murder of the Hon. Ronald Adair by Colonel Moran on 30th March, 1894. Of his dramatic first visit to Watson (Holmes's love for melodrama was too strong to prevent him giving Watson the shock of his life, though he might have expected something of the sort, as he had already thrown Mrs. Hudson into violent hysterics), and the ensuing capture of Colonel Moran, we may all read in the adventure of *The Empty House*, but it is to be noticed that the Colonel escaped the hangman, and pre-

---

[1] Holmes was evidently no mean linguist. He must have spoken, in addition to Arabic, German and French, for his frequent continental investigations would make both essential, and, as we see, he spent some time at Montpelier on his own hobbies, which he would hardly do if he was not at home as regards the language. He quotes, moreover, from German and French authors.

sumably got penal servitude for life, as he was still living in 1902.[1]

Watson was soon induced to sell his practice, and return to Baker Street, and must have been glad to do so. His wife had died the year before, and a change of occupation would be welcome to him. It is clear that the resumption of his life with the great detective was mutually satisfying : ' it was indeed like old times ', he wrote, to find himself once again embarked with Holmes on some mysterious errand, whilst the latter's eagerness to have his old associate back led him to find the money to buy his practice off him.[2] There is an atmosphere about Watson's writings of this period (' The Return ' series) that indicates a thoroughly happy and full life.

Holmes had a busy time all this year : the case of the papers of ex-President Murillo and the affair of the s.s. *Friesland* (in which both he and Watson nearly lost their lives) occurred in May/July, to be followed in August by the matter of *The Norwood Builder*. In November we have recorded the investigation of the death of Willoughby Smith at Yoxley Old Place, and Watson notes a number of other cases, viz. : the repulsive story of the red leech and the death of Crosby the banker ; the

[1] *The Illustrious Client.*
[2] See *The Empty House* and *The Norwood Builder* ; cp. also Mr. Roberts, *Dr. Watson*, pp. 24, 25.

Addelton tragedy ; the singular contents of the ancient British barrow ; the Smith-Mortimer succession case ; and an important continental proceeding, resulting in the arrest of Huret, the Boulevard assassin. For this piece of work Holmes received the Legion of Honour, and was the recipient of an autograph letter of thanks from M. Casimir-Perrier, the French President.

It would appear that the case of *The Second Stain* took place this year, some time during the autumn. Part of Watson's MS. seems lost, for we start in the middle of a sentence, but clearly it must have been prior to *The Bruce-Partington Plans* (1895) since Oberstein was at large in the former case, but got fifteen years in the latter—from about December 1895 or early 1896. Even if he got three months *per annum* allowance for good behaviour, he would be in prison up to 1907. It is curious that Holmes knew the names of the spies in London at the time of *The Second Stain*, but had to get Mycroft to tell him them in *The Bruce-Partington Plans*. Incidentally, since the Kaiser seems obviously the foreign potentate of *The Second Stain*, it must be subsequent to June 1888, when he ascended the throne. As the cause of his irritation was recent colonial developments of England, the ' scramble for Africa ' in the 1890's is probably referred to.

We are, moreover, told that both Prime Minister

and Foreign Secretary [1] called upon Holmes, and as Lord Salisbury combined both offices from June 1895 to 1900, we must be earlier than the former date. The names are, very properly, obscured. Tempting as it would be to read into the pen-picture of Lord Bellinger the personality of William Ewart Gladstone, the chronology will not permit it. Gladstone's fourth Ministry occurred during Holmes's Tibetan travels, and his short-lived third was not in the autumn, but from February to July, 1886. In any case, the adventure being recorded in ' The Return ' series probably indicates that it was after *The Empty House*. Having regard to the various data, it appears reasonably certain that it is Lord Rosebery who is referred to as Lord Bellinger, and Lord Kimberley as Trelawney Hope, and Watson is to be congratulated on his literary skill in hiding their personalities.

The year 1895 was a busy time for Holmes, who, Watson tells us, was never in better form. One of the first cases, *The Three Students*, is of a very peculiar nature. We are not given the precise date, but it occurred during the period of training for the 'Varsity Sports, which suggests early spring —say about March. It seems hardly possible that a later month would suit, as we shall see that Holmes was very fully occupied from April/July,

[1] We presume that the ' Foreign ' Secretary is thinly hidden under the name ' European ' Secretary.

and could not, one thinks, have spared the time then to make researches into Early English charters at the Bodleian Library.

Assuming that about March was the date, we find Holmes and Watson at Oxford (the Quadrangle is expressly mentioned) where the former was engaged upon the aforesaid researches. Possibly he worked at a college library, Watson's acquaintance, Mr. Soames, no doubt being able to smooth away any obstacles to his entry ; but it is a fair inference that no man involved in such researches would fail to utilize the great university library, so rich in manuscripts. We may, therefore, visualize Holmes spending laborious but not unprofitable days in the Bodleian, his work, no doubt, greatly facilitated by Mr. Turner's ' Calendar of Charters and Rolls '. Whether it was work of a private nature or connected with some investigation, we do not know ; at first thought the latter seems more probable, but Holmes did not always devote his energies to business purposes, for later on this same year he prepared and had printed, for his private pleasure, a monograph on the Polyphonic Motets of Lassus.[1] In any case, his work at the Bodleian was absorbing, and he yielded ungraciously to Mr. Soames's entreaties to assist him in the matter of the Fortescue scholarship.

This case has been very minutely scrutinized,

[1] *The Bruce-Partington Plans.*

with most interesting results. As long ago as 1911, Fr. Ronald Knox pointed out [1] (*a*) that it is most unlikely a university scholarship paper should be printed only one day before the examination, (*b*) that it should take the examiner an hour and a half to correct for the press, when it was only half a chapter of Thucydides, and (*c*) that the proofs of the half chapter should be in three consecutive slips. But it is to Mr. Vernon Rendall [2] that we must turn for the fullest criticism. He boldly claims that Watson deliberately hoodwinked Holmes in the affair of the Three Students, with the aid of Soames, Gilchrist and Bannister. Holmes, it is suggested, was worried over his charters, and to prevent his finding solace in drugs, Watson arranged a spoof job for him to investigate. Soames was well known to Watson, who speaks of him as an acquaintance whom he knew ' to be restless in his manner '. Now of the papers for the scholarship, the first consisted of half a chapter of Thucydides. [3] No whole chapter, remarks Mr. Rendall, would occupy anything like three slips of proof matter, nor could Soames take one and a half hours to

[1] *Essays in Satire*, p. 152.
[2] *The London Nights of Belsize*, pp. 147 *seqq.*
[3] Fr. Knox, op. cit., appears to make the mistake of regarding this as the sole material for the examination—' is it likely that a University scholarship paper . . . should consist of only half a chapter of Thucydides ? ' But there were other papers in the examination.

correct (and then not finish) the proofs—he could not have taken half the time. The young man took ' a quarter of an hour, not less ' to *copy* the first slip—i.e. much less time than to correct it ! Further, he was returning from the athletic ground : did he carry with him, when he went down to practice at the long jump, foolscap paper in his pocket, or did he take some of Soames's ? If the latter, had Soames missed any paper from his desk ?—these are questions an investigator should have put.

But why, asks Mr. Rendall, why copy the proofs at all ? Any student sufficiently up in Greek to enter for a University scholarship would take about a minute to get a clue to the passage, which he could then turn up with the aid of his lexicon at his leisure in his room or in a library, without any need to copy it out in a dangerous place. The truth, it is claimed, is that Gilchrist was not really going in for the scholarship at all ; he had the offer of the Rhodesian post in his pocket all the time, and Holmes should have been struck by the suspiciousness of this job being offered and accepted on the *one* night between the cribbing and the discovery without any guardians or relatives being consulted in the matter.

These are very pertinent criticisms, and Mr. Roberts has characterized the theory of a put-up job as ' interesting, though not wholly convincing '.[1]

[1] *A Note on the Watson Problem*, p. 3.

To Fr. Ronald Knox the solecisms in this adventure are one of three lines of evidence that the stories in the collection known as *The Return of Sherlock Holmes* are ' lucubrations of his [Watson's] own unaided invention '.[1] Whilst dissenting entirely from the latter point of view, Mr. Rendall's theory is less easily overgot.

Upon the general theory of a spoof job, we may observe that Watson and his confederates would need to have been consummate actors to humbug Holmes. We have no special reason to think Watson was a good deceiver : on the contrary, Holmes told him that his features were very expressive,[2] and his strongly individual characteristics more than once betrayed him.[3] Again, although Watson was not averse to ' taking a rise ' out of Holmes if he had the chance,[4] his straightforward character and complete honesty do not fit him for any high degree of deception. Moreover, the need of such deception is not established ; so far, indeed, from Holmes appearing to be worried over his charters, we are told he reached some striking results—evidence of success than otherwise.

[1] *Essays in Satire*, p. 154.
[2] *The Cardboard Box*. Cp. his remarks also in *The Dying Detective*.
[3] See *The Hound of the Baskervilles* (Watson's cigarette) ; *The Crooked Man* (habit of carrying his handkerchief in his sleeve) ; *Lady Frances Carfax* (method of tying his bootlaces).
[4] E.g. *The Valley of Fear*—Holmes's reference to Watson's pawky humour.

On the point raised of the needlessness of the culprit copying the paper at all, Mr. Rendall has perhaps overlooked the frame of mind of the cheat. The whole notion of cribbing the examination paper was a sudden inspiration, and we may presume he set to work copying the proofs with equal impetuosity. He was naturally an honourable man, who probably felt hideously guilty the whole time ; he would be in an excited and distraught mental condition and likely to copy hurriedly and blindly, without in any way taking in the sense of the Greek he was engaged upon.[1] To the armchair reasoner, it seems obvious, no doubt, to be on the look out for some striking word, phrase or name, and so to locate the passage by means of a lexicon. The *practised* cheat might think the same, but such self-possession in so dishonourable an act would not ring true of Gilchrist.

Doubtless the copying was done on paper taken from Soames's desk ; the latter would have an ample supply, from which a few sheets would not be missed, and in any case he was in too agitated a state of mind to have known whether any paper

---

[1] Anyone who has done intensive copying will know how the mind tends not to take in what the eye is reading, so that at the end it is necessary to read what has been written to learn what it is really about. The same thing is frequently seen in shorthand writers, who after taking down a number of letters, if asked what the letter to X—— is about, have not even a general idea without referring to their notes. Copying very easily becomes automatic.

had been abstracted, even if Holmes had asked him.

Not very much weight can be attached to the time Soames took in correcting the proofs ; we do not know how, precisely, he spent the time, beyond the fact that he was delayed by the Indian student coming in to speak to him, at which time he had not started on the work (the proofs were still rolled up). This would suggest that Soames had not spent the whole one and a half hours on the task, but had done other things, and indeed, from the ' pitiable agitation ' he got into, he would seem to have been rather an old woman of a man, and such people are apt to be extremely busy doing nothing. As for the quarter of an hour taken by the young man to copy the first page, this was only a guess on Holmes's part, and he was hardly an expert on the time it takes to copy Greek. Moreover, he allowed it was ' not less ' than quarter of an hour, thus permitting it to have been more—as it very probably was.

It is certainly remarkable that Gilchrist should have had an offer of a post in the Rhodesian Police in his pocket at the time, but it is less odd when we remember that his father, Sir Jabez Gilchrist, had been a great racing (and, no doubt, riding) man, to whose son an opportunity for an adventurous colonial life might suitably be offered, and for whom such an existence would be far more congenial than any scholastic triumphs. He had probably had the offer before him some time, and been debating it in his own mind.

As to the unlikelihood of a paper being still in proof the day before the examination, it is observable that only one of the papers was in this condition ; perhaps some last-minute alterations had been made in this paper, necessitating it being set up afresh, hence its being in proof when the others, presumably, were printed and ready. If such were the case, it would be rather a rush job, and possibly it was from this cause that it came to be on three consecutive proof slips. If not, we must confess we do not see a way round a very genuine difficulty that has been raised. We must leave to each critic the task of settling this question for himself ; but having regard to the rejoinders we have entered to Mr. Rendall's other points, and looking to the character of Watson as we know it, we confess we find it more difficult to believe in the hypothesis that the case of *The Three Students* was a 'frame up' than in the canonicity of the events described, possible inconsistencies in the narrative notwithstanding.

In the April of 1895 Holmes had at least two important cases : the peculiar persecution of John Vincent Harden, the tobacco millionaire, and *The Solitary Cyclist*.

During the following three months he was fully occupied. A continental case came before him, for at the request of Leo XIII he investigated the circumstances surrounding the death of Cardinal Tosca, though with what results we do not know. With the arrest of Wilson, the canary-trainer, a plague spot was removed from the East End of London, and there quickly ensued the murder of ' Black Peter ' at Woodman's Lee.[1] Watson speaks of Holmes being frequently absent from their lodgings during the first week of July, in the guise of ' Captain Basil '. We know that these absences were connected with the floating of a spoof whaling expedition, as a trap for the murderer (who would, however, have us use the word ' killer ') of Captain Peter Carey, and, knowing the day of the murder to be a Wednesday in the first week of the month, we seem justified in naming 3rd July as the date of Patrick Cairns's second and fatal visit to ' Black Peter '. It was not, however, till the 10th that Holmes accompanied Stanley Hopkins to the scene of the crime, and laid the unhappy Neligan by the heels. The stupidity of Hopkins in this case has already been referred to.[2]

We are left with a blank record during the remainder of the summer and autumn months, and

---

[1] This case was written out by Watson years later, for he refers to the affair of the Duke of Holdernesse, which was in 1901.

[2] Above, p. 31.

it is not till the third week in November [1] that we encounter Holmes again. It was the third morning of a 'London particular', and Holmes was getting restless at the lack of business. The advent of Mycroft Holmes's telegram came as a relief, and was shortly followed by the great man himself.[2] The body of Cadogan West had been found on the night of the 18th (Monday), and Scotland Yard in the interim had discovered nothing, but merely come to some wrong hypotheses. By the evening of that very day Holmes had solved the mystery, identified the criminal, and subtly inserted the advertisement that was to bring Colonel Valentine Walter to the prison from which he never emerged alive—a striking instance of the great detective's powers. It is true his recognition of the fact that West's body was on the roof of the carriage seems a very long shot in the dark, and one cannot but feel that this was Holmes's lucky day. 'A single blunder on the part of the guilty man would have thrown all Holmes's deductions out of joint'—Father Knox's rather sweeping generalization [3] certainly applies to *The Bruce-*

[1] The actual day of Mycroft's visit was a Thursday—i.e. the 21st.

[2] The adjective cannot be denied to one who, on occasions, *was* the British Government, and whose word, time after time, had decided the national policy. Mycroft's curious position in the Government would seem to have points in common with that of his German contemporary, Holstein.

[3] *Essays in Satire*, p. 166.

Partington Plans. We have already noted the significance of this case for the date of *The Second Stain*, as Oberstein was at large in the last-named, but was 'safely engulfed for fifteen years in a British prison' as the result of spending £5,000 to acquire the submarine plans. The loss of those plans had caused the utmost turmoil in official circles, and the seriousness of the theft may be realized less from the peculiar properties of a Bruce-Partington submarine than from the fact that even Lord Salisbury had been shaken out of his habitual imperturbability. The loss of a very secret report on the possibility of forcing the Dardanelles could leave him unmoved,[1] but Mycroft had seldom seen the Prime Minister so upset as over the Cadogan West mystery.

It is pleasing to know that Holmes's services were not to pass unrequited ; he had himself repudiated any desire to appear in the New Year's Honours List, but the personal gesture of appreciation from the old Queen was probably more gratifying than much public recognition.

We have no precise date for the case of *Lady Frances Carfax,* but certain indications suggest the spring of 1896. Watson was feeling run-down, and took a Turkish bath as a cure—events natural to the seasonal changes that follow the passing of

---

[1] See the amusing account of this matter in *Secret and Confidential*, by Brig.-General W. H-H. Waters, pp. 53–4.

winter. The autumn is possible, but less probable, for Watson grasped eagerly at the chance of a trip to the Continent, and in the autumn the true Londoner digs himself in to hibernate through the winter months. Moreover, a trip abroad is more welcome in the spring than just after the summer holidays. The year might be later, but not earlier, for we have seen how full 1895 was for Holmes, and 1894 is equally out of the question. In 1897 we shall see that his health was in a bad way about March, and he had to go away for a rest cure.

The only other case this year we know of is *The Veiled Lodger*, in the winter, one of those petty items of Holmes's routine work of which we have occasional glimpses.[1]

It is possible that the adventure of *Wisteria Lodge* comes in 1896. It is actually dated 1892, the end of March, at which time, of course, Holmes was believed dead, though really in Tibet. Since *The Red-Headed League* is referred to, the case must be later than 1890, in which case it is later than 1894. It cannot be 1895, for it is impossible to cram it in among the known catalogue of cases in the spring of this year : equally, it cannot be 1897, since in March that year Holmes was a sick man in Corn-

---

[1] See above, p. 66. Watson at this time was apparently on a visit, and not at Baker Street, for Holmes sent him a note asking his attendance.

wall. It might, of course, be any year from 1898–1902 ; we have no sure means of judging.

As already indicated, Holmes's health called for attention in the spring of '97, as the result of his irregular habits (probably including cocaine) and hard work. Dr. Moore Agar ordered him a complete rest, and doubtless enlisted Watson's aid in seeing it carried through. Consequently March found them at Poldhu Bay in Cornwall, and Holmes, with that capacity for switching his mind off on to a fresh subject, was investigating the possibility of Chaldean roots being traceable in the ancient Cornish language. In that secluded spot, however, was to take place the strangest case he ever handled, which Watson did not put on paper till 1910, at Holmes's own suggestion. The fearsome events that engulfed the Tregennis family, and the risky experiment that so nearly cost Holmes and Watson their reason, if not their lives, may be read in *The Devil's Foot*. Here, as in other cases,[1] Holmes shielded the culprit from the rigours of the law, satisfied with the unquestionable equity of his so doing, and in the only other case recorded for this year, *The Abbey Grange*, we find him again ranging his sympathies against the victim.

It is possible that *The Missing Three-Quarter* belongs to 1898, in the month of February. It took place at a time when Watson had succeeded in

----

[1] See above, p. 8.

weaning Holmes away from the drug-taking ' which had threatened once to check his remarkable career '. Surely this last sentence must have reference to the narrowly-avoided breakdown referred to at the time of *The Devil's Foot*? We seem thus to have a time limit before which the visit of Mr. Overton cannot have taken place, but it is of course possible that the year was later.[1] It was only after some years that Watson had cured Holmes of his unwholesome ways, but by the time of the ' Cornish Horror' he was guilty of only ' occasional indiscretions '. No doubt many people have wondered what were the seven different methods which Holmes had up his sleeve for getting a sight of Godfrey Staunton's telegram. To the ordinary mortal it might seem that, had the method adopted failed, the only alternative was to get an official permit. But then Holmes was no ordinary mortal, and had powers that seemed hardly human, as the Duke of Holdernesse was to remark ; if we fail to keep pace with him we must seek the fault in ourselves, ' and venerate where we cannot presently comprehend '.

In the summer of this year occurred the case of *The Retired Colourman*, and from then till 1901 we are left without sure information. That Holmes

---

[1] It was certainly after ' The Return ', for Holmes speaks with wistful longing of the capacity of Dr. Leslie Armstrong to fill the place of Professor Moriarty in the criminal world.

was busy during this time we know well.[1] It is probable that in the period of 1896–1900 we have such cases as *The Dancing Men, The Copper Beeches, Charles Augustus Milverton*, and *The Six Napoleons*, which seem hardly to fit into any previous year.

We ourselves believe that *The Dancing Men* took place in August 1898.[2] Hilton Cubitt's troublous affairs started at the end of June, and he came to Holmes about a month later. The year before, said Cubitt, he had come up to London for the Jubilee. At first sight this should give us the year 1888 for *The Dancing Men*, but in view of its inclusion in ' The Return ' series we are of opinion that Cubitt was referring to the Diamond Jubilee. There is nothing improbable in a man during conversation speaking of the event simply as ' the Jubilee ' instead of by its full title, just as people will speak of being at So-and-so on Armistice Day without meaning necessarily 1918 at all, but some later anniversary. We do not think Watson would include in ' The Return ' collection a story taken from the pre-Final-Problem period of Holmes's career.

The Copper Beeches, we know, is later than 1889,

[1] See *The Solitary Cyclist.*

[2] Extensive investigations locally have not identified Ridling Thorpe Manor, if it still stands, but from such particulars as Watson gives us—seven miles' drive from North Walsham ; within sight of the sea ; some miles from East Ruston—it seems that the neighbourhood of Crostwight is indicated.

as the cases of *The Man with the Twisted Lip* and *The Blue Carbuncle* are referred to. It was before *The Creeping Man* (September 1903), and the season was early spring. Watson appears to be living with Holmes, though it *might* have been one of his frequent short sojourns, in which case 1890 is a possible year. But we are loath to think Watson can have neglected his practice more than is already certain, and we therefore incline to place this case after ' The Return '. The vividly written accounts of *Charles Augustus Milverton* and *The Six Napoleons*, being also in ' The Return ' series, we presume they took place after *The Empty House*. Moreover, Holmes in the former case speaks of Watson and he sharing the same room ' for some years ', and in the latter, Lestrade's assertion that Scotland Yard was not jealous of Holmes, but, on the contrary, proud of him, may be an indication that the bickerings of former times, which had continued as late as 1894,[1] had disappeared with the passage of years. Contemporary with *The Six Napoleons* was the Conk-Singleton forgery case, and some years previously there had occurred the Abernetty murder.

There are three cases which are undated but may fall any time between 1896 and 1902, viz. *The Sussex Vampire*, *The Adventure of Thor Bridge*, and *The Adventure of Shoscombe Old Place*. In all cases Watson was living with Holmes. The first

[1] *The Norwood Builder.*

opens on a 19th November, and, apart from being later than Watson's written record of *The ' Gloria Scott '*, we know nothing of it. *Thor Bridge*, commencing 4th October, appears to be in late years, as Billy, the page boy, is mentioned, and we only hear of him by name elsewhere in *The Mazarin Stone* (1903—see below). The affair of *Shoscombe Old Place* occurred in the month of May ; the fact of its inclusion in ' The Case Book ' series suggests a latish date, as with most others in this volume.

In May 1901 [1] we have the affair of *The Priory School* which is memorable as one of the few occasions where Holmes accepted payment for his services.[2] In this instance, however, the reward

[1] For the benefit of those who may protest that Watson does not mention the year, we may refer them to the following points : (*a*) the year was later than 1900, as the Duke of Holdernesse had been Lord-Lieutenant of Hallamshire ' since 1900 ' ; (*b*) it was earlier than January 1903, the time of *The Blanched Soldier*, as Holmes says he was then ' clearing up the case which my friend Watson has described as that of the Abbey School, in which the Duke of Greyminster was so deeply involved '. Despite the deplorable lapses from accuracy in the names of the school and the Duke (lapses for which, in our opinion, we are indebted to slipshod editorial methods), only one case described by Watson fits the description ; (*c*) Lord Saltire was last seen in school on the night of Monday, 13th May, and a reference to the almanac shows that this can only be in the year 1901.

[2] In *A Study in Scarlet* Holmes speaks of his ' pocketing his fee ' after giving his clients his advice, and of his calling being the means of his earning his bread and butter (see also *The Greek Interpreter*). At a later date, it would seem that he was less dependent on these

had been announced before ever Dr. Huxtable paid his visit, three days after the discovery of the boy being missing—i.e. on the 17th—and there was nothing contrary, therefore, to Holmes's usual principle of letting the work be its own reward. The Duke, when it came to paying, spoke of £12,000 being the sum owed, presumably intending to give the promised reward of £6,000 to Watson as well, unless, indeed, he was hoping to purchase Holmes's silence by doubling the amount due to him. A good deal of discussion has arisen over Holmes's deduction that the bicycle with the patched Dunlop tyre (Mr. Wilder's) was travelling away from the school[1]; the explanation will be found in an article in the *Strand Magazine* for December 1917. It is there pointed out that the depth of the mark of the rear wheel, when the bicycle was going uphill, would indicate the direction of travel, for on the down slope it is very markedly less. In any case, Holmes probably had

fees, and by 1891 he was comparatively affluent, thanks to the King of Scandinavia and the French Government. In *A Scandal in Bohemia*, the £1,000 given him by the King was on account of expenses, and Holmes gave a receipt for it, so he may have refunded any unused balance (something must have been spent in hiring 'everyone in the street' one evening). On the other hand, he remarked to Watson that there was money in the case, if nothing else, the moment he saw the King's brougham. He made £1,000 out of *The Beryl Coronet* transaction. Watson says (*The Dying Detective*) that Holmes's payments to Mrs. Hudson were princely.

[1] See Fr. Ronald Knox, *Essays in Satire*, p. 152.

a dozen other small indications to guide him ; though he might mention only one factor, he usually had others in reserve, as evidenced in the twenty-three additional points of difference in the joint letter of the Cunninghams.[1]

Whether Reuben Hayes was able to see that it would serve his interests to keep his tongue quiet appears a little questionable. One would have thought that, with the scaffold in prospect, he might consider it worth while to do all the harm he could to others, for though it would not help him, it would at least hurt them, and particularly the Duke, for whom he had a strong dislike. It is true he would have to make his damaging statements at his trial, or they were not likely to be made public at all,[2] and to do this would involve admitting his guilt. We must presume that the Crown so presented their case as to leave out all possible mention of the Duke, though one hardly sees how they could avoid bringing in Mr. Wilder's complicity in the abduction of Lord Saltire. If not, Mr. Wilder probably found himself unable to leave for Australia. The reverberations of this case lasted nearly two years, for we have seen that at

[1] *The Reigate Squires.*
[2] There was, of course, no Court of Criminal Appeal then, so Hayes would have no second opportunity of 'splitting' on the Duke, since there was nothing in his case likely to move the judge to refer it to the Court for the Consideration of Crown Cases Reserved.

the time of *The Blanched Soldier* Holmes was still clearing up details.

Simultaneously with this business Holmes was engaged on the matter of the Ferrers Documents, and the Abergavenny murder was coming up for trial.

In June 1902 we have the adventure of *The Three Garridebs*, and in view of some later problems it is worth noting that Watson is still living with Holmes. By September, however, he had moved into rooms in Queen Anne Street, though his association with Holmes had not been broken, for they are found sharing the ' pleasant lassitude ' of a Turkish bath together. This break-up of the Baker Street menage surely indicates that Watson was preparing for that second marriage of which we hear later, and to which reference is made in the Appendix hereto. On the 3rd September came the visit of Colonel Damery, to usher in the case of *The Illustrious Client* (whose identity remains hidden to this day), which Watson, writing ten years after the event, exaggeratedly calls the supreme moment of Holmes's career. Baron Gruner had achieved a European reputation, it is true, but the successful breaking off of his engagement with Miss de Merville can hardly be considered as of prime importance save to the small circle of individuals concerned. If, as Watson is probably implying, it was the exalted standing of the Illustrious Client that gave this case its significance, there could only be one person in England whose position would suit the requirements, and seeing that that person's interests were only involved as a matter of friendly concern, we cannot surely rate this case above the services rendered by Holmes to the nation in *The Naval Treaty*, *The Second Stain*, or *The Bruce-Partington Plans*, or to the royal houses of Holland, Scandinavia and Bohemia. Indeed, from what we learn of Baron Gruner, he was not in the same class as Professor Moriarty or even Colonel Moran, nor did he give Holmes so good a run for his money as did Stapleton. But as we have already observed,[1] the affairs recorded for us in *The Case Book* must be treated with some caution, as seemingly subjected to very unreliable editing.

In January 1903 we have the first example of a case written by Holmes, viz. *The Blanched Soldier*. Watson had at the time of the *Abbey Grange* mystery (1897) challenged Holmes to write up his cases for himself, and had at last succeeded. Moreover, as Watson had just married again, Holmes, rather than be lost, had to be his own Boswell. The Sultan of Turkey's commission occurred at the same time.

The Mazarin Stone, if authentic,[2] and *The Three Gables*, must have fallen in 1903, for Watson was not living with Holmes in either instance. The

[1] Above, p. 42.   [2] Above, pp. 40, 42.

only other case precisely dated in this year is *The Creeping Man* : Watson was summoned by Holmes on the 6th September, and he informs us that this was ' one of the very last cases handled by Holmes before his retirement from practice '. We may conjecture, therefore, that by the end of the year the great detective had laid aside his calling, and it is pleasing to know that many offers were made to settle him on the South Downs with his bees, and even to recommend a suitable house-keeper.[1] His time, Watson says, was divided be-tween philosophy and agriculture,[2] and his bee-keeping bore fruit in the *magnum opus* of his later years, a *Practical Handbook of Bee Culture, with some Observations upon the Segregation of the Queen.* Occasional matters of detective interest came to his notice, such as *The Lion's Mane*, the second and last record written by himself ; but in 1912 the tranquillity of his retirement was rudely shaken. The continual leakage of State secrets necessitated investigation by someone above the calibre of Scotland Yard or the Secret Service, and the Government rightly recognized in Holmes the only man for the job. He was, naturally, not too ready to give up his well-earned peace—be it remembered he was about sixty years of age now, and some-what afflicted by rheumatism [3] —but we cannot

[1] See the *Strand Magazine*, December 1917.
[2] Preface to *His Last Bow*.   [3] See Watson's Preface to *His Last Bow*.

doubt that the persuasive eloquence of Sir Edward Grey went far to break down the opposition which was finally removed under the influence of Mr. Asquith. Holmes went through some exciting and, we may well believe, dangerous experiences before he attracted the notice of Von Bork, and the final laying of the master spy on the eve of the outbreak of the European War was the occasion for the renewal of the old Holmes-Watson alliance that had served the country so well before. No student of Sherlock Holmes can doubt that the years 1914–18 found him hard at work in the nation's interests—doubtless the perspicacity of the genial but anonymous head of the Secret Service [1] secured the willing assistance of one who stood head and shoulders above the common order of men.

[1] Sir Samuel Hoare, *The Fourth Seal*, p. 28 *seq.* Whether Holmes could stand the Secret Service for long is, of course, arguable; it is difficult to see him suffering very gladly the strange medley of affairs outlined, for example, in Mr. Compton Mackenzie's *First Athenian Memories.*

APPENDIX I

1. WATSON'S SECOND MARRIAGE

Mr. S. C. Roberts [1] has lately claimed to have discovered the identity of Watson's second wife, in the person of Miss Violet de Merville, who so narrowly escaped from the clutches of Baron Gruner. We regretfully find ourselves quite unable to accept this conjecture, for the following reasons :—

(1) 'What more natural', asks Mr. Roberts, than that Watson should call upon Miss de Merville after the episode of Baron Gruner was over, to inquire after her health and spirits ? What more unusual, we suggest, seeing that he had never met her. It was Holmes who interviewed her, not Watson.

(2) There is, we think, a certain improbability that a young girl would marry a man of fifty, unless he had very notable qualities.

(3) The social gulf (a larger factor in 1902 than now) would render the marriage still more improbable.

(4) Although Watson had some common experience with General de Merville in the Afghan War,

[1] *Dr. Watson*, p. 27 *seq.*

the unlikelihood of a Regular (and a General at that, moving in the highest social circles) meeting on even terms a retired Army doctor, seems to us very considerable, and still greater the improbability that he would welcome as a son-in-law a man probably close on his own age.

(5) In his concluding remarks, Watson does not know who it was who undertook the task of disillusioning Miss de Merville with the aid of Baron Gruner's book. He could hardly fail to know this if he married her.

(6) Can we really believe that Watson would end the record (written years later) without a hint that he became Violet de Merville's husband?

(7) Watson records Holmes's slightly acid remarks on Miss de Merville's manner ; would he be likely to do so of the woman who became his wife?

(8) Finally, would a chivalrous man like Watson be likely to prepare for publication a full account of an incident which would ever be a shame-faced memory to Violet de Merville, if he were her husband? Surely, she could only wish that the subject was never mentioned again to her ; can we believe a loyal husband would disregard her wish, either in her lifetime or after?

2. BIBLIOGRAPHY OF SHERLOCK HOLMES

Mr. Roberts in the same work gives a list of Holmes's published or projected works. This needs to be supplemented by the following :—

Appendix I

PUBLISHED WORKS

(*a*) ' The Book of Life '—an article in a magazine of
March 1881.[1]

(*b*) Two articles in the *Anthropological Journal* (probably about 1887) on the variability of human
ears.[2]

(*c*) A monograph on secret writings, in which he
analysed 160 separate ciphers.[3]

PROJECTED WORKS

The Art of Detection—Holmes planned to
devote his declining years to composing a text-
book on this topic, focusing the whole subject
in one volume.[4]

It is perhaps worth adding to a bibliographical note
that Holmes refers to his monograph on Tobacco Ash
in *A Study in Scarlet*, so it was probably his earliest work.
It seems likely, too, that the first three at least of the
published works as given by Mr. Roberts were trans-
lated into French by M. le Villard.[5]

[1] *A Study in Scarlet.*
[2] *The Cardboard Box*—see above, p. 61, for the date of this case ;
the articles in question were published the year before.
[3] *The Dancing Men.*   [4] *The Abbey Grange.*   [5] *The Sign of Four.*

APPENDIX II

SIDELIGHTS ON SHERLOCK HOLMES, AS REVEALED IN SOME CHARACTERISTIC *OBITER DICTA*

THIS Appendix does not pretend to be a complete *collectanea* of Holmes's many striking remarks, but merely to throw such light on his modes of thought and action as a cursory survey of his epigrams and maxims may illustrate.

THE ART OF DETECTION

(1) ' There is a strong family resemblance about misdeeds ' (*A Study in Scarlet*).

Compare :

' There is nothing new under the sun. It has all been done before ' (*A Study in Scarlet*) ;
' Everything comes in circles, even Professor Moriarty ' (*The Valley of Fear*).

These remarks suffice to show us why Holmes laid such stress on accumulating that knowledge of sensational literature (' Immense. He appears to know every detail of every horror perpetrated in the century.') that so impressed Watson and Stamford. If you had all the details of a thousand cases at your fingers' ends,

it was odd, said Holmes, if you could not unravel the thousand and first.[1] Many times he impresses this point upon his listeners—to Lestrade, to Gregson, to Inspector MacDonald[2]; and M. François le Villard was quick to acknowledge his indebtedness to the same faculty.[3]

(2) 'It is a capital mistake to theorize before you have all the evidence. It biases the judgment' (*A Study in Scarlet*).

Compare the almost identical remark in *A Scandal in Bohemia*, and :

'It is an error to argue in front of your data. You find yourself insensibly twisting them round to fit your theories' (*Wisteria Lodge*) ;

'We approached the case with an absolutely blank mind, which is always an advantage' (*The Cardboard Box*) ;

'One forms provisional theories and waits for time or fuller knowledge to explode them. A bad habit' (*The Sussex Vampire*) ;

'I make a point of never having any prejudices and of following docilely wherever fact may lead me' (*The Reigate Squires*) ;

'If I had not taken things for granted, if I had examined everything with the care which I would have shown had we approached the case *de novo* and had no cut-and-dried story to warp my mind, would I not then have found something more definite to go upon ? ' (*The Abbey Grange*).

These abundant references to the topic show how keenly Holmes appreciated the liability to form one's

---

[1] *A Study in Scarlet.*   [2] *The Valley of Fear.*
[3] *The Sign of Four.*

suspicions on insufficient evidence. He was not, however, entirely immune from the tendency himself, for both in *The Sign of Four* and *The Missing Three-Quarter* he had to reform his theories, and in *The Yellow Face* his conclusions were definitely wrong.

(3) 'It is a mistake to confound strangeness with mystery. The most commonplace crime is often the most mysterious, because it presents no new or special features from which deductions may be drawn' (*A Study in Scarlet*).

Compare :

'Singularity is almost invariably a clue. The more featureless and commonplace a crime is, the more difficult is it to bring it home' (*The Boscombe Valley Mystery*) ;

'The more bizarre a thing is the less mysterious it proves to be' (*The Red-Headed League*).

(4) 'When you have eliminated the impossible, whatever remains, *however improbable*, must be the truth' (*The Sign of Four*).

This is the most famous maxim of Holmes, and it was a great favourite with him. It is twice uttered in *The Sign of Four*, and we find it repeated almost identically in *The Beryl Coronet*, *The Bruce-Partington Plans* and *The Blanched Soldier*. With it may be compared the remark to Watson in *The Priory School* ; 'it *is* impossible as I state it, and therefore I must in some respect have stated it wrong '.

(5) 'It has long been a maxim of mine that the little things are infinitely the most important' (*A Case of Identity*).

Appendix II

Compare :

'To a great mind, nothing is little' (*A Study in Scarlet*).

'You know my method. It is founded upon the observance of trifles' (*The Boscombe Valley Mystery*) ;

'It is of course a trifle, but there is nothing so important as trifles' (*The Man with the Twisted Lip*) ;

'I dare call nothing trivial when I reflect that some of my most classic cases have had the least promising commencement' (*The Six Napoleons*).

Holmes had, as Watson remarked, an extraordinary genius for minutiæ,[1] and he was always ready to be at any pains to elicit them. 'They say', he observes, 'that genius is an infinite capacity for taking pains. It's a very bad definition, but it does apply to detective work.'[2]

   (6) 'One should always look for a possible alternative and provide against it. It is the first rule of criminal investigation' (*Black Peter*).

Compare :

'When you follow two separate chains of thought, you will find some point of intersection which should approximate to the truth' (*Lady Frances Carfax*) ;

'I should have more faith. I ought to know by this time that when a fact appears to be opposed to a long train of deductions it invariably proves to be capable of bearing some other interpretation' (*A Study in Scarlet*) ;

'One drawback of an active mind is that one can always conceive alternative explanations, which would make our scent a false one' (*Thor Bridge*).

---

[1] *The Sign of Four.*   [2] *A Study in Scarlet.*

(7) ' Never trust to general impressions, but concentrate yourself upon details ' (*A Case of Identity*).

(8) ' Detection is, or ought to be, an exact science ' (*The Sign of Four*).

(9) ' Breadth of view is one of the essentials of our profession. The interplay of ideas and the oblique uses of knowledge are often of extraordinary interest ' (*The Valley of Fear*).

We see in *The Lion's Mane* an example of how Holmes could bring his out-of-the-way knowledge to bear on a problem, and he has a number of interesting remarks on this point in *The Five Orange Pips*.

(10) ' The quick inference, the subtle trap, the clever forecast of coming events, the triumphant vindication of bold theories—are these not the pride and the justification of our life's work? ' (*The Valley of Fear*).

This art was one of Holmes's strongest assets as a detective—he called it the scientific use of the imagination, ' the region where we balance probabilities and choose the most likely '.[1]

(11) ' It is of the highest importance in the art of detection to be able to recognize out of a number of facts which are incidental and which vital ' (*The Reigate Squires*).

No man, not even Holmes, could always be successful in this task, and he recognized the possibility of serious error, as in the remark : ' perhaps when a man has special knowledge and special powers like my own it rather encourages him to seek a complex explanation

---

[1] *The Hound of the Baskervilles.*

when a simpler one is at hand '.[1] Nevertheless, he was inclined to trust his intuitions rather than the surface impressions made by the data of a case—' there is nothing more deceptive than an obvious fact ' [2] —and in a sarcastic phrase he observes, ' all my instincts are one way and all the facts are the other, and I much fear that British juries have not yet attained that pitch of intelligence when they will give the preference to my theories over Lestrade's facts '.[3]

These remarks recall some other comments on matters of Evidence. For example :—

(1) ' There is nothing like first-hand evidence ' (*A Study in Scarlet*).

This truism was carefully borne in mind by Holmes —he was at all times prepared to hear the facts of a case retold to him. Equally he is found ready to relate the points of a problem to a listener, for, as he says, ' nothing clears up a case so much as stating it to another person '.[4]

(2) ' Circumstantial evidence is a very tricky thing ; it may seem to point very straight to one thing, but if you shift your own point of view a little, you may find it pointing in an equally uncompromising manner to something entirely different ' (*The Boscombe Valley Mystery*).

---

[1] *The Abbey Grange.*
[2] *The Boscombe Valley Mystery.*
[3] *The Norwood Builder.*
[4] *Silver Blaze.* We find him adopting the same practice in *The Abbey Grange*, *The Man with the Twisted Lip*, and *Wisteria Lodge*.

Appendix II

Compare :

' When once your point of view is changed, the very thing which was so damning becomes a clue to the truth ' (*Thor Bridge*).

He did, however, allow that ' circumstantial evidence is occasionally very convincing '.[1]

HOLMES AS PHILOSOPHER

(1) ' One's ideas must be as broad as Nature, if they are to interpret Nature ' (*A Study in Scarlet*).

As an instance of an idea of Holmes's as broad as Nature, we may select his theory ' that the individual represents in his development the whole procession of his ancestors '.[2] Watson considered this rather fanciful.

(2) ' How small we feel, with our petty ambitions and strivings, in the presence of the great elemental forces of Nature ' (*The Sign of Four*).

(3) ' To the logician all things should be seen exactly as they are, and to under-estimate oneself is as much a departure from the truth as to exaggerate one's own powers ' (*The Greek Interpreter*).

Holmes was at least guiltless of this failing !

(4) ' Education never ends. It is a series of lessons, with the greatest for the last ' (*The Red Circle*).

(5) ' The example of patient suffering is in itself the most precious of all lessons to an impatient world ' (*The Veiled Lodger*).

---

[1] *The Noble Bachelor.*   [2] *The Empty House.*

(6) ' Is not all life pathetic and futile ? Is not his story a microcosm of the whole ? We reach. We grasp. And what is left in our hands at the end ? A shadow. Or worse than a shadow—misery ' (*The Retired Colourman*).

These depressing reflections are not typical of Holmes, although the tragic might move him to philosophic melancholy, as we see in the Boscombe Valley case, and over the wretched story of Browner in *The Cardboard Box*.

(7) ' What you do in this world is a matter of no consequence. The question is, what can you make people believe that you have done ' (*A Study in Scarlet*).

(8) ' Love is an emotional thing and whatever is emotional is opposed to that true cold reason which I place above all things.'

Again :

' The emotional qualities are antagonistic to clear reasoning ' (Both from *A Sign of Four*).

(9) ' There is nothing in which deduction is so necessary as in religion. It can be built up as an exact science by the reasoner ' (*The Naval Treaty*).

(10) ' To the man who loves art for its own sake, it is frequently in its least important and lowliest manifestations that the keenest pleasure is to be derived ' (*The Copper Beeches*).

Compare :

' The status of my client is a matter of less moment to me than the interest of his case ' (*The Noble Bachelor*).

Appendix II

It is certainly true that Holmes, though no apostle of Equality, and despite the fact that his services were sought by the rulers of many lands, was free from all taint of snobbishness, as evidenced in his epigrammatic comment on Lord St. Simon's fashionably-addressed letter—'this looks like one of those unwelcome social summonses which call upon a man either to be bored or to lie'.

(11) 'It is my belief, founded upon my experience, that the lowest and vilest alleys in London do not present a more dreadful record of sin than does the smiling and beautiful countryside' (*The Copper Beeches*).

Watson was duly aghast at this statement, and we may remember that in *The Final Problem* Holmes blames 'our artificial state of society' for the criminal influences which furnished him with his life's work, a remark which surely attributes a greater meed of blame to urban life than to the more natural conditions in which mankind lives in the country.

(12) 'It is one of the curses of a mind with a turn like mine that I must look at everything with reference to my own special subject' (*The Copper Beeches*).

There is an admirable candour in this recognition of the serious limitations that a specialized outlook may give to the mind's interests. Darwin,[1] we may remember, speaks regretfully of the loss of appreciation of Shakespeare or any poetry which his scientific studies had produced in him, and the student will find some valuable comments in this connection in Professor

[1] *Life and Letters*, vol. i, pp. 100 *seqq.*

Appendix II

Muirhead's *Philosophy of Life*, Chapter VIII. It is recorded of the Victorian judge, Baron Martin, that he seldom if ever read anything but legal works, with the result that when induced to try *Romeo and Juliet* he only commented, ' I find it just a tissue of improbabilities from beginning to end '.[1] So Holmes could speak of Farnham, on the borders of Surrey, as ' a beautiful neighbourhood, and full of the most interesting associations. You remember, Watson, that it was near there that we took Archie Stamford, the forger '.[2]

WOMEN

(1) ' Women are never to be entirely trusted—not the best of them ' (*The Sign of Four*).

It is perhaps open to question whether this ' atrocious sentiment ' reflects Holmes's real opinion. The context in which it occurs suggests he was pulling Watson's leg.

(2) ' Women are naturally secretive ; and they like to do their own secreting ' (*A Scandal in Bohemia*).

(3) ' I have seen too much not to know that the impression of a woman may be more valuable than the conclusion of an analytical reasoner ' (*The Man with the Twisted Lip*).

This remark gives point to Watson's assertion that Holmes, though he disliked the female sex, was a chivalrous opponent, for he tells us in *The Sign of Four*, as we have seen, that he rates ' true cold reason ' above all things.

[1] E. Bowen-Rowlands, *Seventy-two Years at the Bar*, p. 76 *seq.*
[2] *The Solitary Cyclist.*

Appendix II

(4) 'The motives of women are so inscrutable. . . .   Their most trivial action may mean volumes, or their most extraordinary conduct may depend upon a hairpin or a curling-tongs' (*The Second Stain*).

To many a man it might seem that such words embody all the wisdom necessary for domestic life.

(5) 'No woman would ever send a reply-paid telegram. She would have come' (*Wisteria Lodge*).
(6) (The drifting and friendless woman) 'is the most harmless, and often the most useful of mortals, but she is the inevitable inciter of crime in others' (*Lady Frances Carfax*).

Holmes's experience of women was, of course, limited, and perhaps if he had had experience of life in a London boarding-house he might have altered somewhat the first half of this sentence.

MISCELLANEOUS

'Crime is commonplace, existence is commonplace, and no qualities save those which are commonplace have any function upon earth' (*The Sign of Four*).

Compare :

'Life is commonplace, the papers are sterile ; audacity and romance seem to have passed for ever from the criminal world' (*Wisteria Lodge*).
'There are no crimes and no criminals in these days.   What is the use of having brains in our profession ? ' (*A Study in Scarlet*).

We clearly see from these observations that the artist has outstripped the social worker.   Mr. Thomas Burke, we think, has been known to regret the good old, bad old days of Limehouse ; so Holmes, too, could lament the lack of a first-class criminal. ' What we want ', he might have said with H. B. Irving, ' is a good bloody murder '.[1] More than once we catch a wistful tone in his references to the dear departed Professor Moriarty —see *The Norwood Builder* and the tinge of hope that inspired his suggestion that Dr. Leslie Armstrong might fill the gap left by the professor's death.[2]

> ' There is a wonderful sympathy and freemasonry among horsey men. Be one of them, and you will know all that there is to know ' (*A Scandal in Bohemia*).

The emphasis here lies on the words ' be one of them ', for although Mr. Breckinridge was ' horsey ' enough, it was no easy job to learn from him all you wanted to know.[3]

> ' When a doctor goes wrong he is the first of criminals. He has nerve and he has knowledge ' (*The Speckled Band*).
> ' I am one of those who believe that the folly of a monarch and the blundering of a Minister in fargone years will not prevent our children from being some day citizens of the same world-wide country under a flag which shall be a quartering of the Union Jack with the Stars and Stripes ' (*The Noble Bachelor*).

Holmes was in advance of his time in holding these views, and more recent historians of the War of Independence and its causes tend to spread the respon-

---

[1] Compare Holmes's almost bloodthirsty remarks to Watson at the opening of *The Bruce-Partington Plans*.
[2] *The Missing Three-Quarter*.   [3] *The Blue Carbuncle*.

sibility and blame over others besides George III and his Minister. But the idea of an Anglo-American union has not been lost from view, and found favour in the sight of the late Lord Fisher, amongst others.[1]

' Chess—one mark of a scheming mind ' (*The Retired Colourman*).

' There is but one step from the grotesque to the horrible ' (*Wisteria Lodge*).

The definition of the word ' grotesque ' seems to have puzzled Holmes a little. Its element of strangeness and extravagancy did not of itself satisfy his taste. ' One is compelled ', he might have said, ' to find humour and horror linked in the grotesque '.[2]

' To let the brain work without sufficient material is like racing an engine. It racks itself to pieces ' (*The Devil's Foot*).

Compare :

' My mind is like a racing engine, tearing itself to pieces because it is not connected up with the work for which it was built ' (*Wisteria Lodge*).

The first of these remarks is akin to those already noted, which enjoin no theorizing without sufficient data. The second explains his lapses into drug-taking.

' The faculties become refined when you starve them ' (*The Mazarin Stone*).

---

[1] See ' Lord Fisher on the Navy ', p. 26 (reprinted from *The Times*, 13th September, 1919).

[2] Ernst Jünger, *Copse 125*, p. 224.

Appendix II

Compare :

'A concentrated atmosphere helps a concentration of thought' (*The Hound of the Baskervilles*).

If it is true that the English people enjoy a 'frowst' more than others, Holmes was, on unimpeachable testimony, English of the English. Watson awoke at The Cedars to find the room 'full of a dense tobacco haze ',[1] and in *The Hound of the Baskervilles* found Holmes rejoicing in an atmosphere so intolerable that he thought a fire had broken out.

'Some people without possessing genius have a remarkable power of stimulating it' (*The Hound of the Baskervilles*).

Such double-edged testimony to Watson's assistance is only too typical ; a long array of caustic comments on his friend's honest but scarcely brilliant qualities could be culled from Holmes's conversations. Indeed, the very last recorded for us, late at night on the second of August—'the most terrible August in the history of the world '—closed in just such a backhanded compliment. 'Good old Watson ! You are the one fixed point in a changing age.' It was a securely-founded friendship which survived this withering frankness of expression.

[1] *The Man with the Twisted Lip.*

APPENDIX III

THE HOLMES-MORIARTY HYPOTHESIS

A VERY subtle suggestion has been thrown out in private by a distinguished writer whose name may not be divulged. This is, that Holmes and Professor Moriarty were one and the same man ! The essence of this startling idea is contained in the following points :—

(*a*) We have only Holmes's testimony that he and Moriarty were ever together.

(*b*) Holmes was a past-master at disguise ; hence he was particularly capable at playing the part of the Professor, since it called into use his natural interest in crime, but when an inquisitive third person, such as Inspector MacDonald,[1] called, means were taken to obviate any penetration of the make-up by Moriarty sitting with his face in the shadow and the light was turned on the detective's eyes. Had the Professor been undisguised what need had he to take these precautions ? He was a man of some public fame who had occupied a University Chair of Mathematics ; he must, therefore, be known by appearance to many people and he could not avoid the police seeing him more or less any day for he did not pose as a recluse, but as a mathe-

---

[1] *The Valley of Fear.*

matical coach whom one might meet in the street at any time. He could not, in fact, hide his features from the view of anyone who chose to take enough trouble to catch a sight of him ; to adopt a permanent, secret disguise (without changing his name !) would be courting trouble in case he met any of his old colleagues or pupils from his former University. But no explanation is needed of these precautions if Holmes himself was Moriarty, and it is highly suggestive that he should know exactly what reception was accorded to MacDonald.

(*c*) As for the glimpse Watson obtained of Moriarty at Victoria Station or the Reichenbach Falls, there would be no difficulty for Holmes to get one of his associates to impersonate the rôle of Professor, nor was there any risk in doing so, since Watson did not know him by sight.

(*d*) Various other problems suggested by this view, such as the reason for Colonel Moran trying to kill Moriarty at the Reichenbach Fall and in London, are easily explicable. Moran may have fallen foul of Moriarty or have been trying to oust him from his position, so as to grasp the control of the criminal organization himself. Holmes handled the Moriarty affair alone, and Scotland Yard was quite willing to let him do so, and merely pick the plums when ripe. There is no word of Holmes confronting Moriarty with a third person and the various ruses adopted, such as the attempts on his life, were all part of the longstanding plot of hoodwinking police and public with a mythical Professor.

Appendix III

The objections to this view are considerable. In the first place we want to know, is Moriarty Holmes, or is Holmes Moriarty? That is, did Holmes adopt the rôle of criminal in order to break up London's gangsters, much as Birdie Edwards broke up the Scowrers,[1] or did the master-criminal Moriarty, with amazing impudence, adopt an alias as Sherlock Holmes, detective? If the former, the fact would surely be recorded at a later date; the gangsters *were* broken up, and Holmes had no further need to play a part—he could freely talk of the matter to Watson and he must have let the police into his confidence to some extent when he put them in a position to round up the gang.[2] Moriarty was the author of a highly mathematical work, *The Dynamics of an Asteroid*, which was in a class by itself, and he had been a professor at a University in England; could Holmes have played such a part? Could the author of an advanced work on Astrophysics be the man who was ignorant of the constitution of the Solar System? It is true Holmes was quite up to posing as a crook in order to clean up a criminal organization—do we not see him in late years acting the part of an Irish-American in the pay of the German Secret Service?[3] —but when he did so he did not play an entirely lone hand; he always had associates who knew of his impersonation, even in so relatively small a matter as the entrapping of Mr. Culverton Smith.[4] It is simply unthinkable that Watson either should

[1] *The Valley of Fear.* (Readers will not fail to consult the account of this affair in R. W. Rowan's history of the Pinkertons.)
[2] *The Final Problem.*   [3] *His Last Bow.*
[4] *The Dying Detective.*

never know the truth about Moriarty, or if he did should fail to record it—no man could have written *The Empty House* without putting down the facts of Holmes's amazing imposture, nor was there the least reason for Holmes to try to hide up the matter.

Similar objections, only stronger, apply to the alternative theory of Moriarty posing as a detective. He would then have two terribly difficult and risky parts to play. On the one hand he must 'keep in' with Scotland Yard by clearing up crimes for them; on the other maintain his position in the underworld by committing or organizing a vast series of atrocities. Since he was rash enough to tell Scotland Yard all about Moriarty and his gang [1] he would run a fearful risk by committing more offences and a still more fearful one by double-crossing his agents, for, whatever his true character may have been, it is at least indisputable that Holmes landed a lot of men for crimes that the police might never have unravelled. We can imagine a master-criminal who lived in private as a gentleman of leisure, like Raffles; it is possible that he might try and doubly cover himself by choosing such a profession as a detective; but would he not be careful to be a detective of very ordinary qualities rather than court the limelight as the outstanding persecutor of crime of his day? On general grounds alone the whole notion is too fanciful; can anyone really imagine such a Pooh-Bah of crime, who as Lord High Murderer could so hide his traces that as Lord High Detective he could not discover the authorship of the deed? Was it this

[1] See *The Valley of Fear*.

Appendix III

retiring mathematical don of ascetic tendencies whose straight left sent ' a slogging ruffian ' home in a cart [1]; was it the confidant of Kings and Statesmen who had been driven from his University town by the dark rumours that had collected round him; was it this Napoleon of crime, the master forger, robber and murderer,[2] whose sensitive gorge rose at the very thought of the master blackmailer? [3] Why did not Colonel Moran, whose enmity can only be explained on the assumption that he had learned how Moriarty had been intriguing with the police, give him away? How can we equate the 'Varsity careers of Holmes and Moriarty, the one absorbed in desultory chemical studies, the other winning European favour in mathematics at the age of twenty-one? The more we reflect on this Holmes-Moriarty hypothesis the more we are convinced that it is adequately answered in Holmes's own words : ' it seems to have only one drawback, and that is that it is intrinsically impossible.' [4]

[1] *The Solitary Cyclist.*   [2] *The Final Problem.*
[3] *Charles Augustus Milverton.*   [4] *Black Peter.*